THE RUNWAY DECADE

THE
RUNWAY
DECADE

Building a Pre-Retirement
Flight Plan in Your Fifties

BILL BUSH, CRPS®
& PETE BUSH, CFP®

HORIZON
M E D I A

THE RUNWAY DECADE
Building a Pre-Retirement Flight Plan in Your Fifties

ISBN   978-1-5445-2698-0   *Hardcover*
       978-1-5445-2696-6   *Paperback*
       978-1-5445-2697-3   *Ebook*

This book is dedicated to you.

Not you right now as you are reading this, but you at your retirement party. Older you. Future you.

There are a lot of wonderful people counting on that version of you, and on behalf of all of them, we tip our hat for making this a priority.

CONTENTS

INTRODUCTION

"The best time to plant a tree was twenty
years ago. The second best time is today."
—Ancient Chinese Proverb

Entering a new decade in life feels a little bit like passing a
road marker on the highway during a long drive.

"Oh, hey, kids, we just entered a new state! Look at that!"

It's not just another year, it's a whole new stage of your
life. Your teens give way to your twenties, and not far into
that decade, you become a legal adult, forever leaving
behind the alibi of, *"Give him a break. He's just a kid!"*

When you reach thirty, you wake up one day and realize that you have subscriptions you don't use, a growing

401(k) balance, group life insurance, and to your parents' amusement, an acute awareness of the fact that you're getting older. "Wow, where did my twenties go?" you wonder. "I'm a fully responsible adult all of a sudden, with a family and a career and bills to pay."

Then you hit forty and realize you've basically *become* your parents. You awake on your fortieth birthday to find black balloons decorating your yard. "Aren't those for old people?" you think. You have a mortgage, your kids are growing up, and you're gradually climbing the ladder in your career. Hopefully, you're also accumulating a bit of money, saving, and making smart long-term decisions. Still, retirement feels like it's far off in the future.

But when you reach fifty, retirement becomes very real for the first time in any meaningful way. It's not so far away anymore! If anything, it's now looming on the horizon, and you can actually see it in the distance. At this stage, you have friends and co-workers who have retired, you're probably an empty-nester or close, and your parents, if they're still with you, are in their senior years, probably dealing with health problems. And there are more black balloons in the yard. This time, you get it.

With retirement so close now, you start to worry about how you're going to spend the rest of your career preparing for it. Is it too late? Are you on track? Do you have enough time left? Can you possibly retire early, or will you have to retire late?

"My gosh, it feels like half my life is over," you lament.

Statistically speaking, you're not wrong. The average expected lifespan of a man born in 1967 is 79.67 years. For a female, it's 83.23.[1] If we round that number off, it means the average fifty-year-old has about thirty years of life left.

Since Americans generally retire around age sixty-two, when Social Security first becomes available, that means the average fifty-year-old only has twelve years until retirement. After retirement, those statistics say the average person will live another eighteen years or so before making their "final landing." With fifty-plus years in the rearview mirror, twelve, eighteen, and thirty years seem to pale in comparison.

Bear in mind, these are only averages, and they include people of all shapes, sizes, genetic makeups, and health profiles. The simple fact that you're reading this book suggests that you're probably better educated than the average person, which also translates to better health education and choices. You've likely parlayed that education into earning an above-average income and had greater opportunities to build wealth.

---

1   Social Security Administration, Period Life Table, 2017, https://www.ssa.gov/oact/STATS/table4c6_2017.html.

Those averages also include all of the people who died young, never making it to fifty, which brings overall life expectancy down. When you add all of those up, with education and wealth being highly correlated to longevity, you have a host of good reasons that you can expect—and need to plan for—a longer than average lifespan. Consequently, depending on where you are in your fifties, you might only have a handful of active earning years left to get your finances in order to provide you and your family with a reliable income stream that will last for twenty, twenty-five, or thirty years or more in retirement.

It's a daunting prospect, isn't it? If that scares you even a little bit, you are not alone. In fact, if you have no idea how much money you need to be able to comfortably retire and *stay* comfortably retired regardless of life's twists and turns, you are *definitely* not alone. Almost everyone has a sum of capital that is needed to replace their monthly living expenses in retirement, but very few know what that number is. And it may be bigger than you think.

Chances are, you already have a 401(k) or other retirement plan in place, and maybe you've accumulated some other savings and retirement benefits, like a pension or Social Security. But even if you've saved well and done all of the things you're supposed to do as a responsible working adult, the road to retirement can still seem unclear from where you stand in your fifties. How do you accurately project forward what it will all be worth, and how in the world do you take this future sum of money you'll have accumulated and turn it into an income stream that's going to last for the entirety of your retirement years?

Retirement income planning focuses on having a dollar-specific, date-specific strategy for covering your expenses when the regular paychecks stop coming in. It can be an intimidating process, so it's understandable why going through that transition will be one of the most stressful times in your life. At this stage, are you sure you'll have enough money to survive, much less thrive and live the kind of retirement lifestyle you've always dreamed of? Having a few fragments of a plan, or a general idea of the path ahead, isn't really enough. While there's no shortage of information, education, and calculators online at your fingertips, somehow you have to sort through the clutter, figure out what is relevant to you, and then create a very specific and personal roadmap that's going to get you to and through retirement successfully.

RUNNING OUT OF RUNWAY

Here's the good news: you still have time! We call the fifties "the runway decade" because you still have time in your working life to set yourself up for a successful retirement. While you should be well on your way to accumulating the resources you'll need, there is still runway left if you are behind or just starting to focus on it.

It's not too late, but you *do* have to start creating that clear, concise plan right now. Sure, when an airplane makes its turn onto the runway for takeoff, the other end looks very far away, but once the plane gets moving and momentum builds, the runway gets shorter and shorter rather quickly. Like the plane, your pre-retirement life is already barreling down its own runway, and there's no time to waste. Just as you peer out of a plane's window and see lights and reflectors zipping by at increasing speed while taking off, so do the days, weeks, and *opportunities* seem to pass by in your own life. If there was ever a time to take action, it's now.

People we meet in their late forties and fifties usually have a lot of questions about retirement planning, and you've likely had similar thoughts yourself. We hear these kinds of questions and others all the time:

- How much will I need, and how do I know if I'm on the right track?
- How much should my money grow to if I just keep doing the same thing I'm doing?

- Do I need to put away more for retirement, or can I enjoy life a little more right now?
- Am I investing in the right things for my goals, risk tolerance, and time horizon?
- Should I pay off the mortgage faster or save/invest more for retirement?
- What role should I expect Social Security to play in my retirement income and when is the best time to take it?

In this book, we want to help you by motivating and encouraging you to develop a holistic financial plan with clear steps that will lead to your desired retirement lifestyle. To do that, we're going to share with you the very same process that we take our clients through. We call it **The Confident Wealth Experience®**, and it's going to clarify the pieces of your roadmap and give you the confidence and sense of direction you need to be on the path to retiring well.

Our hope is that this process will get you to the point where, when you wake up in the morning and put your feet on the floor, even though you may have a few things to worry about on a given day, your financial and retirement planning won't be among them. When you can see clearly where you're going and feel confident about the road ahead, that confidence has a ripple effect throughout the rest of your life: relationships, work, decision-making, everything. It's practically a superpower.

But, as we said, there's only a limited amount of runway to take off, so it's wise to start taking action now. Life moves fast and, as the old saying goes, "Time is money."

Can you imagine what life would be like if you were forced to retire today? Would you be ready? Even if you've accumulated substantial personal savings, are you confident it's enough to last the rest of your life? And in your fifties, you wouldn't be able to draw Social Security or access your retirement accounts yet, which are typically the two biggest sources of retirement income for most Americans. You might be in real trouble.

Fortunately, you're not retiring today. You have runway left, so there's still time to check the gauges, adjust your direction, and push the throttle forward to full confidence.

WE'RE IN THIS TOGETHER

All of these things hit close to home for both of us because we happen to be in our mid-fifties. Like you, we're right in the middle of the runway decade, headed toward take-off, and we've lived through the same world events and life experiences that have shaped both *the* world and *our* world.

LIFE EVENTS YOU'VE PROBABLY EXPERIENCED BY YOUR FIFTIES

- You or your spouse changing careers
- A business sale or acquisition
- Attending a friend's or classmate's funeral
- A personal health scare
- Your spouse's health scare
- Gaining weight and having less energy
- A divorce and splitting of assets
- A step up to a higher tax bracket
- Your peak earning years
- Dealing with more complicated tax issues
- Placing a parent in a long-term care facility
- Refinancing your house, moving to a new house, or paying for big repairs/updates to your old house
- An unexpected financial setback that burned through savings
- Kids going to college or graduating
- Getting close to paying off your mortgage
- A child needing "launch" money
- Empty nest
- Celebrating a silver anniversary
- One or both parents passing away
- Children getting married
- Becoming a grandparent

WORLD EVENTS YOU'VE LIVED THROUGH
(IF YOU'RE IN YOUR FIFTIES)

- The Civil Rights Act
- The Equal Rights Amendment
- Man walking on the moon
- Presidential assassinations and attempts
- The Bicentennial of the United States
- Inflation
- Milli Vanilli
- Black Monday on Wall Street
- The end of the Cold War
- Recessions
- The dot.com boom and bust
- 9/11
- The growth of the Digital Age
- The 2008 Financial Crisis
- The first black President of the USA
- Shifting back and forth between a Democrat majority and a Republican majority
- The first female Vice President

The world we live in today is different than the one we were born into, and the one we retire in will certainly be different still.

While we can never control what goes on in *the* world or *the* future, we can focus, plan, and prepare to make improvements to *our* world and *our* future. Professionally, over the past thirty years, we've served thousands of people through our wealth management and retirement plan businesses, helping them create roadmaps for their future financial well-being.

Not only do we help other people navigate this stage of life, but we're navigating it ourselves. That gives us both a professional and personal perspective on the runway decade. We see the struggles that clients face, and we're feeling the emotional impact ourselves.

We know what you're going through, and we certainly take our own medicine when it comes to planning. We also know some things you need to start doing to get ready for retirement right now that may not even be on your radar yet. In the following chapters, we're going to walk you through many of those things. To be clear, we're not providing specific individual recommendations. It's simply not possible to do that in a book.

Although this book is packed with useful perspectives and information, it is not intended to be a replacement for the personalized one-on-one advice that can only come from a relationship with someone who understands the nuances of your specific situation and circumstances. It's also not a replacement for your common sense but hopefully can serve to strengthen it. In that respect, please consider this a useful guide as you seek to establish the solid team of financial advisors you'll need to rely on as you progress down the runway.

Instead, we're going to look at the broadly applicable ideas that everyone in the runway decade needs to be thinking about. By the end, you'll have the perspective you need to start creating your own roadmap to retirement, so you'll be able to provide, protect, and prosper for the people who are counting on you.

It all starts with figuring out where you want to go.

WHERE ARE YOU GOING?

"If you don't know where you're going,
you'll probably end up someplace else."
—Yogi Berra, New York Yankees Catcher

I magine sitting at your future retirement dinner at your favorite restaurant, in a private room with your spouse, adult kids, and a few grandkids, along with some close friends and other important people from your professional life. Everyone is congratulating you on a great career, and at some point, your best friend raises a toast with a nice glass of the sommelier's recommendation of the house's best wine.

"Enjoy retirement, my friend," they say. "You've earned it!"

As the emotion of the moment wells up inside of you, your spouse squeezes your hand and gives you that comforting smile that you know so well. Your mind flashes back a handful of years to the age you are today, and you recall the decisions made, the gratification delayed, and the journey that got you from this moment to a place of confidence about retirement. Looking back, what did that journey look like? What did you have to do between now and that future retirement dinner toast in order to feel happy and excited about the end of your career? What burning questions did you have that you got answers to, and what were some of the risks you had to factor in?

If you're a business owner, maybe you had a great exit from your business and you sold it for the number you envisioned that left you in a comfortable financial position. If you're a physician, dentist, or attorney, maybe you successfully groomed the next generation to leverage your time and ultimately acquire your practice.

Or perhaps, like many successful people, you rose to the top of your company or profession, earned a great income, built a plan, and simply saved and invested additional money to build a bigger nest egg and create a better retirement income stream. Regardless of your path and personal details, you can look back proudly on the choices you made, and maybe more importantly, the ones you *didn't* make.

Now you're back to the future, receiving the toast from your best friend. Your mind starts to drift forward as you think about all of the things you want to do, the places you want to see, and the memories you want to make with the people you love. This is your picture of life in retirement, in as vivid a color as you can dream it up. Where will you go? What will you be doing when you wake up each day? What have you put off that you now have time and freedom to get to? This is *your* vision of your retirement, so dream big.

We call this "writing the history of the future," and it's a crucial first step in planning. You have to see it first. In client conversations, we often share a couple of quotes that were ingrained in Pete's brain while playing college baseball at LSU for legendary Hall of Fame Coach Skip Bertman. Coach Bertman used these quotes to get a bunch of eighteen- to twenty-one-year-olds to win multiple NCAA College World Series Championships in his career.

The first one is the classic Paul J. Meyer quote: "Whatever you vividly imagine, ardently desire, sincerely believe, and enthusiastically act upon, *must* inevitably come to pass." The second is a well-known quote from William Johnsen: "If it is to be, it is up to me." The former is about believing in a big future, and the latter is about who has to make that future a reality. You get to decide, and you have to see it first.

We know this sounds like a pretty basic message that you have probably heard over and over: Decide what you want, when you want it, and what you need to do and are willing to do to get it. That's just Goal Setting 101, right? We agree! The problem is, few people actually do it, and that's especially true when people are planning for retirement. Almost the entire population stumbles forward and takes whatever circumstances the universe dishes out to them, and then asks themselves, "How did I end up *here* instead of *there*?"

Kudos to you for picking up this book. Just by taking that step, you've put yourself in motion toward developing, or maybe just refining, your vision and financial goals. Motivational speaker and sports psychologist Dr. Kevin Elko has said, "You either live in vision or in circumstance." Translation: You get to choose your mindset. Choose vision.

While most people can easily pick numbers as goals that represent progress from where they currently stand, numbers by themselves will fail to inspire you when challenges arise. Pictures and visions are great as well, but even they can be hard for others to grasp and may seem a little "out there" to you or your family, who might accuse you of dreaming too big.

The best approach is probably some combination of the two: not just the measurements and milestones you want to strive for, but the qualitative factors as well. What will it feel like, why do you want it, and what does your ideal retirement look like? What will you do for fun to celebrate the wins along the way, and with whom will you celebrate? As we have said on many occasions, "You can't chest bump yourself," so make sure to include your family, friends, partners, or team in your vision.

Maybe there is no right way to do it, but what has worked best for many people is to mentally put yourself into that future time like we did earlier at the retirement toast and use your imagination to think vividly about what has to be true for you to feel happy, accomplished, confident, and successful with what you've experienced between now and then. In a sense, you really are writing the history of the future the way you want it to be, and just like any other type of creative writing, the more detail you use, the more those images will sear themselves into your unconscious mind where they can be worked on even while you're sleeping.

This is a key distinction to grasp. You aren't projecting forward what you *hope* happens or what you *wish* possibly *could* happen. You are, in fact, writing in past tense about what has *already* happened because you've put yourself into the future and are now turning around, looking back, and telling the story about what you experienced. We don't know why or how, but this makes it real in a way that simply thinking and planning forward does not.

It's beginning with the end in mind, and since we're sticking with the runway theme, isn't that exactly what an airplane pilot does? They know what their destination will be and their checklists ensure that they think backward to every detail that will allow them to take off and land that plane safely. As they head down the runway, they're focused on the precise steps required to ensure that the plane gets off the ground and on course successfully.

No competent pilot heading down the runway looks over to their co-pilot and says, "Hey, where should we take this thing?" or "What happens next? I guess we'll figure it out as we go!" Would you get on that plane? No, of course not.

In the same way, you need to be thinking very specifically about the moment of retirement that you are headed toward and not leave it up to chance. This is yet another reason why we called this book *The Runway Decade* because runways and decades both end at some point down the line. It's time to put the end in mind and start planning accordingly.

IT'S YOUR JOURNEY, NO ONE ELSE'S

A successful retirement is a personal journey. What you're working toward, what you want, and the path to get there will be different from other people. You set your destination, then you work backward to determine the right path to get there.

It's easy to get caught up in how friends, co-workers, or family members are approaching retirement or to have media messages suggest what your retirement should look like. If you've ever seen a picture of a gray-haired couple holding hands and walking on a beach or a golf course, or riding on a sailboat, or fishing with a grandchild, you know what we mean. There's nothing wrong with any of those things if they interest you, but they should only serve as a catalog of choices for how you *might* want to spend your time and resources in retirement.

If you're anywhere in your fifties, you probably remember the old *Sears Wishbook* catalog that used to come in the mail every year just before Christmas. We have vivid memories of excitedly flipping through the latest copy, picking out all of the toys we wanted and daydreaming about Christmas morning.

Just like almost everything else these days, you can find and flip through old copies online. For a fun stroll down memory lane, we recommend it, especially with your siblings! We enjoyed reminiscing about our nine- and ten-year-old selves as we flipped through the 1975 *Sears Wishbook* online recently. G.I Joe with Kung-Fu grip? Circle that in green ink. The Six-Million Dollar Man action figure? Check. A disc jockey phonograph set on page 612? Double circle! It certainly stirred up the imagination (and more than a few laughs).

That's how you need to feel about your retirement. Yes, there are some factors you have to take into account. For example, as kids growing up in a family with six children, we were pretty sure Santa's budget was tight. There were some expensive toys in the *Sears Wishbook* that we knew we'd never get. At the same time, we weren't afraid to dream big and circle the ones we liked, even though we knew there was a chance that Santa might not come through. We're talking to you, Cyclone Power Jet™ Air Hockey table. It was called a "wishbook" for a reason!

This kind of thinking is crucial for a successful retirement, but very few people do it. There's a reason that the first thing a GPS asks you is, "Where do you want to go?" In an instant, it goes out "there" and looks back to where you are to determine the most efficient path forward. Many times it will give you options to pick from.

The same will likely be true with your retirement, because for each choice you make, there is usually a trade-off. By this age, most people have accumulated some money in savings and are adding to it on autopilot, but they're mostly just drifting toward retirement and hoping for the best without any idea of what they will need. Think about it like this: If you get in your car and see that your tank is half full, the question, "Do I have enough gas?" is answered with, "Where are you going?" Similarly, when people ask us if we think they will have enough saved for retirement, our answer is usually the same: "Where are you going, and what is it that you want?"

Retirement comes along just once in your life, and it takes years of careful preparation to get it right. While there is still runway left, you can gain confidence by selecting your destination, planning your path to get there, and preparing for potential problems you might face along the way. We will cover the problems in detail in the next chapter, but first, with healthy doses of both optimism and realism, we want you to begin by visualizing your ideal scenario if all goes as planned.

Your destination and path don't have to look like anyone else's, but you need to gain clarity on them in order to inform the actions you will need to take to get there. In our experience, while some overlap and rhyme with one another, everyone's situation is different in the details, and what you need to do to prepare now for retirement will be unique to your desires and intentions.

Think of it this way, with the "magical" city of Orlando representing retirement. Let's suppose you and your cousin are both set to arrive in Orlando at the same time, but you're coming from Baton Rouge, and he's coming from Newark. The flight path you're each going to take will vary significantly, as will the traffic patterns you face along the way, the weather you'll have to deal with, the people you're traveling with, the flight crew, and the amount of fuel you will need to comfortably reach the destination and land safely.

It's the same "retirement" destination, but a very different plan to get there. And even when you both arrive, the differences magnify. He may want to play golf while you head to the theme parks. These differences will be even more dramatic, of course, if you and your cousin are headed to completely different cities.

For that reason, the very first step in achieving a successful retirement is to clarify your destination. That means very specifically defining your ideal vision of retirement. Don't worry, you may get a chance to re-dream it later when you have more actual information about how things turned out. Think of it like having a wide range of focus based on projections and estimates that narrows over time as you get closer and obtain more facts.

The scope of possibilities will narrow as you approach retirement and know what you're dealing with. But it's better to have a vision and adjust than it is to have no vision at all. What will your retirement have to look like in order for you to be truly happy?

Of course, one essential element of happiness is eliminating financial anxiety and worry. Your journey might differ from others, but that's one thing every successful retirement has in common. Granted, by this stage of the game, you have come to realize that money may not be able to buy you happiness, but true happiness sure is hard to achieve if you're constantly worried about money.

Just like putting a puzzle together, it helps to "paint in the edges" first to give your vision a frame to work from. To do that, you need to answer some basic questions for yourself, such as:

- Where do you want to live? Will you need to downsize or relocate?
- What kind of housing situation do you want? Will you have a yard to keep up with?
- Will you have your mortgage and other debts paid off by retirement?
- What do you want to do with your time? What are your main hobbies and what do they cost?
- Do you want to take regular vacations? Where to and how often?

- Will you want a vacation home? If so, where and will you want to rent it out when you are not there or just enjoy it with family and friends?
- Are there charitable causes you want to support financially or with your time and talent?
- Do you want to provide for your grandchildren's education?
- Do you see yourself having an encore career, consulting or working as you want to?

Only you can answer these kinds of questions for yourself, because you are the only expert on you. Only you know what's going to make you happy and fulfilled during retirement. We will discuss in more detail in later chapters how to determine if you are on the right track and if you will have enough, but it will all come back to what you need and want, what it will cost, and how much you'll need to comfortably retire.

Much like our circles in the *Sears Wishbook*, some of the things you want might seem impossible right now. But if you're fifty years old, you could have twelve to fifteen more years of work and income to help you accomplish them. For example, if part of your vision for retirement is to buy a vacation home in Florida so you can spend part of the year by the beach, you may not be able to afford it right now, but it might be possible in the future if you make a plan and start funding it.

In other words, don't assume that something won't be possible at retirement just because it's not possible now. This is the time to dream. As you get closer to retirement, you can adjust your expectations if you have to, but for now, create the ideal that you're shooting for, so you know exactly what you're working toward. Then head off in that direction.

Sure, there will be adjustments along the way, just like you'd have to adjust the sails to the wind on a sailboat. You would never point your boat toward a destination and then go down below the deck to play cards and hope to arrive safely. As you are faced with various conditions on the journey, you adapt and adjust. Your retirement plans will be no different, but as we said, you might just find that you can adjust your dream as you go and re-dream even bigger.

Now, you may be thinking, "I don't know what I'm going to want in fifteen years. That's a long way in the future!" The truth is, it's really not that far away, and it will get here quicker than you imagine. Just think ten or fifteen years into the past. Where were you, how old were your kids, and what was going on in your life then? Doesn't it seem like yesterday? Chances are, the next fifteen years will feel like they are moving even faster. Things move fast on the runway.

Have you ever noticed those little words on your side mirror in your car: "Objects in the mirror are closer than they appear"? It's one of those sayings we see practically every day. While it's intended to be a reminder for drivers about things appearing behind them, when it comes to retirement planning, if you could turn that mirror around, it might say something like, "Objects in the *future* are closer than they appear!"

In other words, life comes at you fast. In order to put yourself in the right frame of mind to figure out what you want for your retirement, it's helpful to remove yourself from your current busyness.

Today is filled with to-do lists, work deadlines, bills to pay, and family obligations, among other things, but there's nothing yet on your schedule ten, twelve, or even fifteen years from now. It's a blank slate, and you can mentally draw whatever you want on it. Pull out a blank piece of paper and just start dreaming. Write down ten to fifteen specific things about your ideal life in retirement, using questions like the ones we provided above.

It's important to capture why each specific thing is important to you, as well, because it's the "why" that keeps you motivated to achieve the goal. Since goals are just "dreams with a deadline," decide when you want each goal to be accomplished. For example, if you write, "I want to own a lake house within a two- to three-hour drive from our home," you might then write, "To have a place to make special memories with family and friends," as your "why." Maybe you decide you want this to be true by the time you turn sixty years old, and your first action is to determine a general location and an approximate amount you'll want to spend.

Whatever the specifics are for you, there's power in writing these things down as you begin to clarify your vision for retirement. For a sample "Retirement Goal Planning" worksheet, visit *www.runwaydecade.com.*

FACTORS AFFECTING YOUR VISION

Even though we've told you to dream big and make your retirement vision *your own*, there are some factors that may affect your decisions.

- **Spouse:** If you're married, your spouse absolutely needs to have input on your ideal retirement vision. Dream it up and fill out the goal worksheet together. Like many things in your journey together, you will each see retirement through your own lens. Your spouse may have their own retirement benefits and decisions to factor in as well. You might want different things, in which case you'll have to find a compromise that you can both live with.

- **Social Security**: If you're in your fifties, you can probably trust that Social Security will still be available by the time you retire, so don't forget to include that financial resource into your future income plans. However, to minimize the impact of future legislative changes on your retirement income plans, it is wise to build your own nest egg to produce the income you will need. While it should be there in some form or fashion, use the mantra we shared earlier: "If it is to be, it is up to me." If you're reading this and you happen to be much younger than fifty, you should make your plan as though you will not be able to count on it.

- **Age/Years of Service**: Depending on the type of retirement benefits you've accumulated, your age and years of service can come into play as well. Early retirement may or may not be an option, depending on the specifics of your plan and your income needs. If you're fifty, you have a good bit of runway left. However, if you're already fifty-nine, your runway is shorter, and you don't have as much time left, especially if you're starting with very few financial resources. Adjust your vision accordingly.

- **Health Insurance:** If you plan to retire earlier than sixty-five, when Medicare coverage begins, you will need to consider how your healthcare needs will be covered in the interim. Some group benefits are extended to retirees until age sixty-five, or you may need to purchase your own coverage to fill the gap. Healthcare is one of the higher inflationary categories, so this could be costly.

- **Expenses:** Remember that some expenses you have now will go away in retirement. The money you are saving in retirement accounts each month, for instance, will no longer be part of your income needs. Ideally, your mortgage and other debts will be paid off as well, further reducing your overhead. A long-held rule of thumb in the financial industry suggests you may need somewhere between 75 and 80 percent of your pre-retirement income to live comfortably after retirement.

- **Discretionary Income:** Keep in mind that your future goals will be funded from the funds you choose *not* to spend today. You are delaying gratification to store up reserves for a time when your paychecks stop. As you dream optimistically, you must also be realistic about what part of your income is truly discretionary. If your job only pays enough to provide the basics, you're probably not going to be able to store up enough savings to buy a retirement home in La Jolla with an ocean view. At the same time, if there are things you are spending on today that you'd be willing to sacrifice for a better tomorrow, your big dreams may actually be reasonable and achievable. Morgan Housel put it this way in his recent book *The Psychology of Money*: "Wealth is hidden. It's income not spent. Wealth is an option not yet taken to buy something later. Its value lies in offering you options, flexibility, and growth to one day purchase more stuff than you could right now."

- **Business Owner:** If you're a business owner, or have a professional practice of some kind, you need to include a business succession plan in your vision for retirement. What are the options in your industry for your exit strategy? Do you have partners and other stakeholders to consider in your plan? If you're like most business owners, your business is likely your biggest investment, with much of your net worth tied up in the business. Do you know how much the business is really worth and what levers and metrics drive its value to a buyer? Some owners overestimate the value of their business, and when you're close to retirement is not the ideal time for a reality check.

- **Family**: You might also have a family situation that affects your retirement. This could include kids, parents, extended family, and so on. Do you anticipate having elderly parents to care for? Did you have children later in life who you expect to still be caring for in retirement? Do you have a close family member with special needs who you're responsible for? Take a look at the chart below to start thinking about how old everyone will be and what they might need when you are ready to retire.

In essence, most people are striving for their own version of what Dan Sullivan, founder of Strategic Coach, calls *The Four Freedoms*: freedom of time, freedom of money, freedom of relationships, and freedom of purpose.

A GLIMPSE OF THE FUTURE

As a helpful exercise, create a list of the most important people in your life, their current ages, and how old they will be every five years into the foreseeable future. Try to imagine where they'll be at the time of your retirement, and what you expect their life circumstances to be by then. This gives you a glimpse of the future that you can use to frame some of the thinking about your retirement vision. For example, is it likely that your children will be out of school, living on their own, and taking care of their own needs? Is it likely that your parents will be alive and need help, financial or otherwise?

	Current Age	Age in...		
		5 Years	10 Years	15 Years	20 Years
You				
Spouse				
Child 1				
Child 2				
Parent 1				
Parent 2				

To download your own copy of "A Glimpse of the Future" table, visit *www.runwaydecade.com*.

If you are an entrepreneur of any kind, we encourage you to dig deeper into this concept and many others at *www.strategiccoach.com*.

He frames it differently for business owners, but loosely translated for non-entrepreneurs, you are striving for a retirement that gives you the ability to spend your time as you see fit, have enough money and income sources to live comfortably without working, spend it with the people you want to be with, and fulfill a sense of purpose and meaning along the way. If you can nail those four things, it would be hard *not* to be happy in retirement.

As Yogi Berra famously said, "If you don't know where you're going, you'll probably end up someplace else." In regard to your retirement, if you don't figure out what you want to accomplish, you won't be able to create a path for getting there. Bear in mind, this retirement vision isn't carved in granite. You can adapt and change along the way, just like a pilot might change course once they're in the air if they run into bad weather or air traffic.

Your mission now is to get motivated and intentional about retirement and point yourself in the right direction. You've dreamed big and considered various factors that impact that vision. Now, it's time to think about the obstacles that lie ahead and come up with a plan for dealing with them.

OBSTACLES TO OVERCOME

"You either pay the price of discipline,
or you pay the price of regret."

—Dr. Kevin Elko

"I've been meaning to call you guys for three years, and just never got around to it. But now I can feel the clock ticking, and I wish I'd started meeting with you when I was a lot younger. I'd probably be in a lot better shape for retirement."

We hear things like this all the time following a first meeting with a prospective client. So many people in their fifties regret things they either did or didn't do and all of the lost time that they could have used to prepare for retirement. As you think about your ideal retirement lifestyle, as you *dream big*, you may have similar regrets, but the truth is:

Regret solves nothing.

All you can do is use the past for learning and make sure three years doesn't become four, five, or six years! Waiting for the "right" time is pointless. Feeling regret over lost time is no reason to lose more time! That's a bit like our business friend who was complaining about how hard it was to find someone with three years of experience to fill a position in his company. When we asked him how long he had been searching, he said, "Five years." How much further ahead would he have been if he had just hired and trained someone?

You might have said to yourself, "If I could have just started planning sooner," or "If I wouldn't have wasted that money," but you can't go back and change any of that. As our mother used to say, "If *ifs* and *buts* were candy and nuts, we'd all have a Merry Christmas!" All you can do is start taking action now and move forward from here.

More time might have given you different choices, but that doesn't mean it's too late to start making more deliberate and meaningful progress toward your retirement goals right now. The very fact that you're reading this book shows that you're already getting serious about planning for your future.

Regardless of where you are on the runway, or whether you have saved a lot or a little, the point is to avoid the mental trap of *thinking* about planning for retirement, but not acting on it. Not knowing where to start, putting it off, feeling anxious about it, being afraid of making a mistake, and putting it off some more won't get you to your big dream.

Although we will cover other common obstacles, problems, and challenges to overcome in this chapter, this hits on perhaps the biggest obstacle of all: *procrastination.* Overcoming inertia and taking the first step often unlocks the motivation and forward motion needed to reach your goals. And if this book is about anything, it's about motivating you to move your financial planning to the front of the line. As the ancient Chinese philosopher Lao Tzu stated, "A journey of a thousand miles begins with a single step."

THE ROAD TO SUCCESS ISN'T A STRAIGHT LINE

Unfortunately, there's another quote that applies here, and it's from the Scottish poet Robert Burns: "The best laid plans of mice and men often go awry." Just as life itself isn't a straight path, the road to a successful retirement is never a straight line. You will encounter forks in the road and unexpected detours, where tradeoffs and difficult decisions have to be made.

Plans "often go awry" because of some common culprits that you have likely already encountered on your journey up to this point. And they will continue to inhibit your progress down the runway unless you identify them, anticipate them, and develop strategies for overcoming them. We will dive into them in more detail, but as we do, be honest with yourself about how these have affected you so far:

- Putting things off: good old-fashioned procrastination
- Too busy with a hectic life, work, family (i.e., not enough time)
- Frozen in fear: scared of making a costly mistake or doing the wrong thing
- Being disorganized and not realizing it costs you money and opportunity
- Things used to be simple, but as you have grown, they have become complex
- Lack of knowledge or interest in financial things
- Too much noise and industry jargon make things confusing
- Need help but don't know who to turn to or trust
- Not paying attention to your personal savings rate

- Not knowing where your money goes: details of expenses and outflows
- Not having a margin of safety of cash for emergencies
- Carrying too much debt or not having a plan for paying it off before retirement
- Not working off a plan: you've just been figuring it out as you go
- Cookie-cutter plans overlook personal nuances in your situation
- Changes in your family dynamics or career opportunities
- Factoring in your emotions around financial planning
- Not understanding the difference between the risk of permanent loss and volatility
- Understanding that investment success is predominantly behavioral

While this is certainly not a comprehensive list of problems you have faced or will face along the way, some combination of these and other challenges is constantly working against you to keep you from reaching your financial goals. Identifying your biggest worries, fears, and dangers reveals what is standing in your way and where to focus your energy to create immediate progress.

MAKING PROCRASTINATION YOUR FRIEND

Procrastination is the direct result of the ambitious goals you've set for yourself. If you didn't want something bigger, better, or different, there would be nothing to procrastinate about! For example, if you decide you want to buy a retirement home on the beach within the next five years, you're setting yourself up to confront some specific obstacles along the way simply because you want it. You have to figure out the ideal location, the size of the house you want, local taxes, insurance, and how to come up with the down payment and financing for what will likely be an expensive goal.

The devil is in the details, and the details likely include things you've never dealt with. Eventually, you'll run into something outside of your areas of knowledge, or you might be too busy to deal with it all and get stuck. Maybe you'll just need more feedback or confidence that you are on the right track and making a good decision.

Similarly, maybe you've put off looking at your asset allocation in your 401(k) account, or haven't gotten around to updating your will, or increasing your life insurance coverage. All of these are areas you might want to improve, but most people procrastinate on important things like these because they simply don't know how to take that first step confidently.

In their book *Who Not How*, Dan Sullivan and Dr. Benjamin Hardy lay out the foundation for overcoming procrastination. It's easy to get stuck when you approach a task or goal due to a lack of time, knowledge, or skill, but if you shift your mindset from *how to make progress to who you can turn to for help*, you will skip over the frustration and delays straight to the solution. If you look hard enough, there is always a "who" for practically any "how."

The shortcut to making procrastination your friend when it comes to long-term planning is to simply ask yourself what specific thing you are procrastinating about and why. Then name the reason you're stuck and who you can turn to for help.

For example, you might say, "I have put off updating my will, but I need to get it done because it's been ten years, my kids are all grown, and so have my assets that I would leave them. I'm confused about how to best structure things at this stage of the game. Therefore, I will ask my brother, my advisor, and my business partner for three good referrals to a good estate attorney."

MAKING TIME

Yes, life can be hectic and come at you fast, but the truth is you already make time for everything that's important to you. Don't you? To overcome the challenge of being too busy and never having enough time to focus on your finances or long-term plan, build the time into your system and protect it.

Start small, perhaps with an annual update or review in the summer, over the holidays at year's end, or whenever you know that the calendar won't be as full as normal. Put it on your calendar and schedule it like a meeting. Enlist an accountability partner if needed. This could be your spouse, your financial or tax advisor, or a friend or family member you trust. Approach it as you would your annual health checkup and make it one of the most important meetings you set with yourself each year. The most successful people we know all have systems for regularly reviewing their financial matters regardless of the frequency or schedule.

FREEZING IN FEAR

Fear can be motivating, like running when you see a snake or leaving town ahead of a hurricane (those two are personal for us), but it can also be paralyzing and keep you from making decisions that would help you move forward in life. Inappropriate responses to fear can mean *not* taking some sort of action that you should or taking some action that you *shouldn't*. This is especially true when it comes to financial decisions because, as social scientists and behavioral economists Daniel Kahneman and Amos Tversky discovered, humans are about twice as averse to the pain of loss as we are to the excitement of gain.[2]

The more your wealth and assets grow, the more costly it can be to make a bad decision. If you only have $10,000 saved, then a 10 percent mistake costs you $1,000, but if you have $1 million dollars, a 10 percent mistake costs you $100,000. That's a big difference, so you can see why people get scared.

You may be brilliant in all kinds of ways, but we've seen many smart, talented people freeze in their tracks when it comes to financial matters. They may choose to stay parked in cash (which produces a negative real return after taxes and inflation are factored in) because they fear the stock market is "too high" or "too volatile" or "too risky" to invest in at the moment because of _____ (fill in the blank with the current crisis, such as an election, debt ceiling, or recent market correction).

More often than not, people invent things to be scared of, whether it's the boogeyman under the bed or the fear

2   Daniel Kahneman and Amos Tversky, "Prospect Theory: An Analysis of Decision under Risk," *Econometrica* 47, no. 2 (March 1979): 263–92.

of investing. Situations usually turn out way better than we imagine because our reptile brains are still programmed to protect us first and foremost. Along those lines, we regularly remind our clients of what Mark Twain said: "I've lived through some terrible things in my life, some of which actually happened."

If you discover that fear is holding you back because you worry about the impact of your decisions, you need to determine if your fear is real or imagined, rational or irrational. Maybe you can gain confidence from research, or maybe you need to seek out an alternate perspective from someone you trust to help you think it through. It's okay to admit you're stuck—that just makes you human—but don't stay frozen long, because it's also perfectly human to admit you need help.

THE DANGER OF BEING DISORGANIZED

Simply put, being disorganized can cost you money and opportunity. Not only can it result in unnecessary fees, payments, and expenses, it can keep you from taking advantage of a prospective financial win. Much like "making the time," it's about paying attention to the details.

When you're not tending to the details, money is probably leaking out. Back in the mid-nineties, there was an ad running in magazines for a well-known investment company that featured a big, cartoonish guy strolling down a winding path with a backpack over his shoulders. Unbeknownst to him, the road behind him was littered with coins and dollar bills that had fallen out of a hole in his backpack. Imagine for a moment that the backpack represents your entire financial life, and the money on the ground is all of the unknown costs that slowly and insidiously slip away each week, month, or year. That's what we mean when we say money is leaking out.

Figuring out where money is leaking out of your financial life and plugging those holes will put more money back toward your retirement and other financial goals. We've seen examples where plugging holes saved people thousands of dollars, but even if it only saves you a few hundred bucks a year, that still adds up. If you're leaking $500 a year through fees and lost opportunities, that adds up to $7,500 over fifteen years, not counting what it could possibly earn for you.

What if it were $5,000 per year or even $10,000 per year? Wouldn't it be nice to have that additional money for your big vision in the previous chapter? Wouldn't you at least like to know how much it is?

So what are some of the common ways to look for these leaks?

One common leak comes from changing jobs. The average person changes employers four or five times during their professional life, which can create a string of fragmented 401(k) plans. We've seen clients who had multiple retirement plan accounts from previous employers they left behind, and besides not being watched or coordinated, each of them was charging higher fees than their current employer's plan. If this shoe fits you, depending on the size of your accounts, you could be looking at substantial savings each year. It's at least worth looking into, isn't it?

Another one we don't see quite as often now that interest rates have been so low for so long is unnecessary mortgage interest or interest charges on other debts, such as loans or lines of credit. Available rates in the marketplace change constantly, so it makes sense to evaluate your options to see if you can reduce the amount of interest you pay to banks or mortgage companies.

Perhaps one of the biggest areas where money is leaking out is on your tax return. We make it a point to review every client's past couple of years of tax returns, and as a result, we have found missed opportunities to reduce their tax bill through lost deductions or simple mistakes. Many times, opportunities are missed to actively offset gains and losses before year-end, resulting in higher capital gains taxes being paid.

Not fully funding tax-deductible retirement accounts, incorrectly calculating taxes on certain stock grants, or even improperly accounting for Roth IRA conversions have all been examples of tax dollars leaking out. Sometimes you can amend your return and get them back, but sometimes they are lost forever. It's always best to be proactive before year-end when it comes to any form of tax planning.

Other places to look are unnecessary or outdated insurance premiums on old policies you may not even need anymore, high investment management fees, bank charges, or subscriptions you no longer use. Believe it or not, even failing to update your beneficiaries on retirement accounts or insurance policies can force money to leak out to the wrong person at the wrong time. It's better to know right now and take action!

Last, you might have lost property out there somewhere that you've forgotten about. Certain states have lost property databases that you can search. It's not a bad idea to look. Is it possible that you have old savings or investment accounts that you've lost track of because you moved or changed jobs? Even if the account only has a few hundred dollars in it, that's still money you could put toward something worthwhile, like your retirement.

While there may not be anything you can do about the past, you certainly don't want to get five, ten, or fifteen years down the road at retirement, look back, and see a trail of money you missed out on going as far back as the eye can see. Plugging the leaks is all about getting organized.

COMPLEXITY AND CONFUSION CREEPING IN

Several common obstacles revolve around things becoming complex that were simpler at one point. As your financial life evolves and your wealth grows, you naturally acquire more moving parts, which ushers in more complexity.

You're probably an expert at what you do for a living, but that doesn't always translate into being knowledgeable about everything you need to do with the money you earn from your job. It could be that you just don't have as much interest in studying financial matters. Or perhaps you find finances intimidating and tend to avoid them until absolutely necessary.

If you really want to become a financial expert, there's a massive amount of information to ingest, enough to fill entire libraries, and quite frankly, most people don't enjoy spending their weekends reading about finance. They have families, hobbies, and other obligations to consume their time. It turns out there's a good reason why becoming a professional financial advisor can take years of study and an official certification.

The process of getting clarity about your money can indeed be confusing, complex, and intimidating, and the media doesn't always help. To be fair, the financial industry doesn't make it easy either. This industry is rife with jargon and terminology that can make your head spin. It's hard to get precise answers to even basic financial questions, and all of the jargon creates a bunch of mental noise when you're trying to plan for your future financial needs.

The stock market changes constantly, tax laws get rewritten every year, and you're inundated with advice from financial websites, TV and radio shows, and podcasts. A lot of the free advice you get from so-called financial experts might provide you with some good general tips and information, but it can't speak to the nuances of your specific situation. Furthermore, there is just so much advice coming from so many people that it sometimes feels impossible to sort it all out and know how it applies to your life.

That's why we always use plain speech and the type of conversational language found in this book when we sit down with clients. We want to cut through the veil of industry terminology that obscures things for most people.

If you're a self-reliant person, it can be hard to admit you need help figuring out your own financial future. On top of that, with all of the negative news around bad actors in the financial industry, it can be hard to know who to trust even if you do decide to use a financial advisor. And just because you sit down to talk to a professional doesn't mean you'll automatically feel comfortable getting "financially naked." Peeling back the layers of your life to examine your money can be as hard as baring your soul to a therapist. First, you have to feel comfortable trusting someone with every part of your financial life. Then, you have to trust that they're going to provide the right guidance.

If you're a guarded person by nature, this can be a struggle, and on top of that, we've all read the stories about shady financial "experts" taking advantage of clients, running Ponzi schemes, or charging exorbitant fees. Even though those bad actors are very rare, they get a lot of media play, which can ramp up the anxiety. But there are also plenty of caring and trustworthy advisors to vet.

The media doesn't tell heartwarming stories about people who retired successfully and then quietly enjoyed the rest of their lives. No, they tell the horror stories that make it hard to trust anyone. So, when you finally meet with an advisor, it's natural to wonder, "Do I really trust this person enough to hand all of my money over to them? If they take advantage of me, everything I worked so hard to accumulate could just evaporate forever."

Fortunately, there are organizations like FINRA and the SEC that offer ways for you to check the backgrounds of industry professionals and their firms. While services like these aren't foolproof, they can at least help you narrow down the field of candidates a little. In our opinion, it's worth the time and effort to find the right financial advisor. Working with a trustworthy financial advisor could help provide clarity on any gaps in your own financial knowledge, and help ensure that you are getting a retirement plan that is tailored to your specific needs. This is something the free online retirement calculators and infographics just can't do for you!

We've talked to clients who have put off coming to us because they're frustrated or embarrassed that they couldn't figure it out all by themselves, saying things like, "Why does retirement planning have to be so confusing? It should be simpler and easier."

We partially agree. It *should* be easier. But if you rise above a certain level of wealth, you can expect "simpler" to give way to "complex."

KNOWING YOUR NUMBERS

One of the best ways of staying financially confident and organized is to keep up with your important numbers. When you're in your peak earning years, you tend not to be as concerned about where every penny is going, but in retirement, you will need to be crystal clear about your budget since you'll be living on a fixed income. That's why it's important to get a grip on your cash flow and budget right now.

It's advisable to pay attention to the two basic financial statements that communicate in real time how you are doing financially. These two basic interrelated financial reports are your Income Statement and your Balance Sheet.

Your Income Statement simply shows all sources of money coming into your household and all sources of expenses going out for a specific period of time (e.g., monthly, annually). When done properly, it accounts for every penny you've earned and spent, even if some of the spending was putting money into savings and investments. This report is good to look at monthly so you can keep your finger on the pulse and make timely adjustments as needed.

Your Balance Sheet, on the other hand, is a summary of your assets and liabilities. It summarizes everything you own and everything you owe. Your house, car, personal belongings, savings and investment accounts, business interests, and more are all listed under your assets. Your mortgage, car loan, lines of credit, and other money you owe are listed as your liabilities. When you subtract everything you owe to others from everything you own, you get your net worth.

These two reports are interrelated and work together to determine your financial solvency. It is the excess cash from the Income Statement that allows you to save and invest, purchase real estate, and grow the numbers on your Balance Sheet. But when you retire and the work income stops, many (though not all) of the expenses will continue, making it important to have a reliable retirement income plan in place. When it works out well, the Balance Sheet assets can be structured to produce some or all of the income you'll need to cover expenses once your paychecks stop.

The Income Statement is supposed to feed and support the Balance Sheet, but without a well-thought-out plan, this can get flipped around. Once your assets on the Balance Sheet (savings, investments, business interests, real estate, etc.) begin to be sold or liquidated to feed the Income Statement to cover monthly expenses, it is simply a matter of time before you are broke. When all of the assets have been sold to meet liabilities or supply income on the Income Statement, it's "game over." As the old saying goes, "If your outflow exceeds your inflow, your upkeep becomes your downfall." It has also been said that "cash is king," but the truth is, cash *flow* is king.

In essence, you should look at the assets on your Balance Sheet not in terms of their value, but in terms of how much income they can produce. In other words, don't think to yourself, "I have a million dollars"; instead think, "I have a million-dollar asset that can produce $40,000 to $50,000 per year in income."

Knowing these numbers helps you determine what percentage of your income you're saving each year, which in a lot of ways is the crucial number. Again, from Morgan Housel in *The Psychology of Money*, "Building wealth has little to do with your income or investment returns and lots to do with your savings rate."

Think about it like this: If you make $100,000 and save 1 percent of your income, you'll save $1,000. If your friend makes $40,000 and is able to save 10 percent of their income, they will save $4,000. You may never have thought of it in those terms, but if you find yourself behind on the runway, now is the time to get a little more aggressive about practicing delayed gratification.

Doing so will allow you to increase your personal savings rate and accumulate more for retirement, but it can also help you build your cash reserves to create what we refer to as a "margin of safety." Having cash on hand for emergencies or the unexpected twists and turns of life is always a good idea, and it will help you avoid having to go into debt. Furthermore, entering retirement with at least two years' worth of income needs in liquid savings or cash creates a buffer against needing money and having to sell shares when the market is down.

Closely monitoring your numbers also provides you with information about whether it makes sense to accelerate debt payments in order to go into retirement debt-free. Ideally, you want to enter retirement without carrying *any* debt because you'll want to control expenses when you're on a fixed income. If you can take care of all of your debts before your last day on the job, it will have a huge impact on your ability to fully enjoy retirement. There is something peaceful and calming about not having loans, credit card debt, or a mortgage hanging over your head when you're no longer earning a steady paycheck.

You start to get a handle on your debts by looking at the fixed and variable expenses on your Income Statement. Fixed expenses are things that have a minimum payment you can't change, usually contractual obligations like mortgages and car loan payments. Your variable expenses include things like dining out, clothes, and vacations. If going into retirement free of debt is as high on your list as it should be, consider which variable expenses you can reasonably cut in order to increase the principal payments above the minimum on your fixed expenses.

The Income Statement and Balance Sheet are two pieces of an overall financial plan that can serve as your guide as you approach retirement. Many people just drift forward and figure it out as they go, or use some sort of cookie-cutter planning tool that doesn't factor in their specific details. Neither of those will give you the confidence you are looking for heading down the runway.

You can find a sample Income Statement and Balance Sheet at *www.runwaydecade.com*.

CHANGES WITH FAMILY AND CAREER

If your parents are still alive, have you considered the possibility that you might have to contribute financially to their long-term care at some point? It's a good idea to have a financial conversation with them now, if you're able to. Unfortunately, people rarely discuss this issue with their parents until it becomes an immediate problem.

Granted, it's not an easy conversation to have. We recommend making time over lunch or coffee and saying something to your parent or parents like, "I was doing some financial planning for myself, and my advisor asked me a question that I didn't know the answer to: 'Do you expect to have to provide care, financial or otherwise, for your parents at some point?' We don't have to talk about it right now, but we probably should at some point when you're ready. As we do our planning, it will be good to

INCOME STATEMENT

Income

After-Tax Salaries and Wages	$350,000
Investment	$3,125
Other Income	$11,500
INCOME AVAILABLE	**$364,625**

Less: Savings Buckets

Retirement Plan Contributions	($54,000)
Additional Investing	($24,000)
HSA Contribution	($8,300)
Rainy Day	($12,000)
Taxes	($9,000)
TOTAL SAVINGS	**($107,300)**

Less: Living Expenses

Housing, Mortgage, Rent	($30,000)
Transportation	($32,400)
Groceries	($15,600)
Utilities	($11,400)
Travel and Entertainment	($21,200)
Insurance	($19,500)
Other Debt Payments	($6,000)
Other Expenses	($33,200)
TOTAL LIVING EXPENSES	**($169,300)**

NET INCOME / DISCRETIONARY $88,025

PERSONAL BALANCE SHEET
as of January 20_ _

ASSETS

Cash and Equivalents

Cash and Checking	$85,000
Savings - Discretionary	$45,000
Savings - Taxes	$75,000
Savings - Vacation Home	$65,000
Other Cash Assets	$0

Liquid Investments

Brokerage Accounts	$750,000
Retirement (Deferred)	$1,500,000
Other Investments	$0

Private Equity $250,000

Real Estate

Primary Residence	$1,200,000
Investment Real Estate	$225,000
Other Real Estate	$550,000

Personal Property $435,000
(Automobiles, boats, furnishings, jewelry, etc.)

TOTAL ASSETS $5,180,000

LIABILITIES

Short-term Liabilities

Current Upaid Balances	$12,000
Credit Card Debt	$5,500

Long-term Liabilities

Mortgage Loan	$800,000
Auto Loans	$65,000
Other Debts	$125,000

TOTAL LIABILITIES $1,007,500

NET WORTH (ASSETS - LIABILITIES) **$4,172,500**

Securities and advisory services offered through Cetera Advisors LLC, member FINRA/SIPC, a Broker/Dealer and Registered Investment Advisor. Cetera is under separate ownership from any other named entity.

know about your financial circumstances so we can be there to help and factor them into our plans. No rush or pressure, but I just want you to know I'm ready when you're ready."

This might disarm them a little bit, especially if they don't like talking about finances in the first place. You won't sound like you're just probing for information about your inheritance, and even if they're not immediately ready to discuss it, you've at least opened the door to revisit the subject soon.

You want to avoid reaching retirement and suddenly discovering that your parents lack the money to provide for their own long-term care needs. Otherwise, you might find yourself spending another several thousand dollars a month to provide for their care at a time when you need it most.

The goal is to minimize surprises, because, as one of our longtime industry mentors, Nick Murray, has said, "Surprise is the mother of all panic." While no one likes unpleasant surprises, panic can lead to actions that destroy wealth.

Beyond your parents and their future financial needs, what else are you worried or anxious about today that you don't want to be worried about at retirement? Think carefully through each component of your life, not just your financial life. What are the conversations you're having with yourself or with your significant other that are nagging at you, demanding a solution?

Maybe your kids are still in need of support, or maybe you're concerned about job security. Maybe you need to readjust the amount of your salary going into your 401(k), cash savings, and investments. Maybe you just wonder if you're invested properly for your goals, or maybe you haven't looked at projections of what it could all be worth at retirement.

Do you need to have a power of attorney in place for your elderly parents or healthcare directives for yourself? Perhaps you worry about having enough life insurance or long-term care insurance between now and retirement, or you worry if your will is going to reflect your most current wishes. If you own a business, you might need to decide on your transition or exit strategy.

If you can make even just a little bit of progress in dealing with your biggest worries, you will gain a lot of confidence about your retirement planning. What are some of the things you need to do that you've been putting off? Only you know what these things are, and it's best to get them out of your head and onto paper so you can get the answers you need to move forward.

OVERCOMING YOUR OWN EMOTIONS AND BEHAVIORS

As you do this exercise, pay attention to your emotions around some of these topics. One of the biggest obstacles you have to overcome when planning for retirement is your own emotions and related behaviors. Some of these emotions are deep-seated and hard-wired into your psyche, based on what you witnessed or heard your parents say about money as you were growing up. Some come from experiences you've had along the way, and some come from things you've read or been told by the media.

When most people think of financial planning, they think in terms of logical decision-making about investments, dividends, interest, tax deductions, and so on. While the investments and other financial products and strategies deal with the logical side of the brain, financial planning is typically more of an emotional process. The products and services in the industry are like a doctor's tray of tools during a surgical procedure. For the most part, they just lie there on the tray until someone puts them to use to solve a problem. As a patient, you don't really care about scalpels, clamps, and gauze pads; you just want your problem diagnosed and fixed.

The same is true with your financial matters. In other words, you don't necessarily want a long-term care policy; you just fear (an emotion) depleting your family's resources if you need around-the-clock care at some point. You don't really want to go visit with an attorney to get your will done; you're just worried (an emotion) that your children might squander their inheritance, fight over it, or get taken advantage of if you don't protect them. You don't necessarily even want investments, but you do want the security and protection that they can afford you.

As Harvard Business School Professor Theodore Levitt said, "People don't want to buy a quarter-inch drill. They want a quarter-inch hole!"

You're going to find yourself navigating an emotional minefield full of fears and anxieties as you plan for your financial future. However, letting your emotions guide your behavior and decisions can lead to some huge financial mistakes. You won't see them as mistakes at the time, because our emotions make us rationalize things that we might later regret. We've seen emotional decision-making produce some real financial train wrecks, so that's why we're putting an emphasis on this as an obstacle early on.

Along these lines, it will be important to examine your thoughts about what you believe. Thoughts guide your emotions, emotions guide your actions, and actions determine your results. Perhaps Dan Sullivan said it best when he said, "The problem is never the problem. The problem is that you don't even know how to think about the problem."

MISTAKING VOLATILITY FOR PERMANENT LOSS

For some people, the biggest worry is the performance of the stock market. They're worried about losing all of the money they've invested if the market experiences a significant downturn. This is usually the result of not understanding how the market works, not knowing the historical trends, or not having clarity about the volatility of their investments.

We'll dig into more of the details in Chapter 7, but we want to address it here as an obstacle, because this lack of understanding can be an impediment to achieving long-term financial goals like planning for retirement.

OBSTACLES LEAD TO SOLUTIONS

As you can see, this is a big chapter, and there are many obstacles you have to overcome in order to achieve a successful retirement. But don't get discouraged. Every obstacle that you face contains the raw material you need to move one step closer to long-term financial success.

During your runway decade, try to identify as many obstacles as you can and take action to move past them. Since you can't "read the label from inside the jar," get an outside perspective to make sure you turn over every stone. Chiefly, this means getting clarity on exactly what your money is doing right now and making adjustments to get you where you need to be when you retire. Even if you still have a lot of work to do, you will start to feel a lot more confident about your future the moment you decide to take action.

Some of the difficult decisions you face will be the result of unexpected events. No one can predict the future perfectly. Just as there have been in your life already, there are bound to be some surprises in the future, and a few of those surprises might impact your retirement plans. Sometimes, overcoming problems is a bit like Hercules fighting the nine-headed Hydra. Every time you cut off one head, another one rises to take its place. That's why it's best to set your expectations to revisit your plan frequently.

The point is, you don't just create a retirement plan, set it in motion, then sit back and ignore it for fifteen years. There are going to be obstacles along the way that you have to confront, and some of them may require some difficult decisions. At times, because of unforeseen circumstances, you will face a fork in the road where you have to figure out which way to go. But if you know where you're headed in the first place, those decisions become easier.

By deciding on your vision and anticipating the potential obstacles along the way, you are already on your way to eliminating the possibility of arriving at retirement full of regret. But like any great trip, you have to know exactly where you are starting from.

WHERE ARE YOU NOW?

"To know thyself is the beginning of wisdom."
—Socrates

erhaps you've participated in that most American of pilgrimages: a family vacation to Walt Disney World. If you've visited "the world's biggest mousetrap," then you know how vast and complex it is. With several theme parks and water parks and an enormous shopping/ dining district, it can be a challenge to find your way around.

And, of course, there are numerous "must-see" attractions that must somehow be experienced within a limited time frame. This requires some careful planning and a lot of running around. A single wrong turn on the way to Space Mountain, and you might find yourself stuck in a thirty-minute queue for Goofy's Barnstormer.

Fortunately, there are several tools to help guests navigate this massive jungle of joy. First, there are guidebooks written by independent experts who have painstakingly figured out every little detail of visiting Disney World. They can tell you what time of day to ride specific rides, when and where to watch parades and fireworks, and which trash can to throw your Mickey Ice Cream Bar wrapper into.

Disney parks also provide maps to help you get your bearings. Some maps are printed, some are available in the Disney Parks app, and others are displayed prominently in the parks themselves. So, if you don't know the lay of the land and your kids say they want to ride Space Mountain *right now*, you have a clear process for figuring out how to get there.

What is that process? Well, you need to obtain three pieces of information from the map. First, you need to locate Space Mountain. This might take a moment. It's the big white building on the far-right edge of the Magic Kingdom map. Second, and just as importantly, you have to figure out where you are. The printed maps can't tell you that, but the posted maps will often include a small red triangle that says, "You are here." Once you've identified these two locations—where you are and where you want to go—you can figure out the best path to get your desperate kids to Space Mountain.

Your financial planning works much the same. As we've already discussed, the first step is clarifying where you want to go, but once you've done that, you have to figure out exactly where you're starting from. It's the only way to identify the most efficient path for reaching your destination.

WHO YOU ARE TODAY

There are many roads to long-term financial success, but before you can find the right road, you have to identify the "you are here" of your financial life. For some people, that can be an unpleasant experience, especially as you confront the consequences of your past decisions or mistakes. It's a little bit like lifting the rug in your living room to see all of the accumulated dust and debris you've swept under it over the years.

Just remember the words of Ralph Waldo Emerson: "Finish each day and be done with it. You have done what you could. Some blunders and absurdities no doubt crept in; forget them as soon as you can. Tomorrow is a new day."

Yes, you've probably made some financial mistakes and blunders. You missed some opportunities by reacting to fear and doubt, but it's a new day. The purpose of clarifying where you are now is not so that you can lament the past. It's so you can start taking the right steps toward your destination today.

That requires taking an honest and total inventory of your current financial state. There's no getting around this, but understand that what you see in your finances today doesn't represent who you are today. You're actually looking at the results of who you were in the past. Decisions and behaviors from your past have created your present financial circumstances, whether good, bad, or ugly. Those decisions may have put you in great shape today, but if not, they don't have to define your future.

You get to decide who you are today and who you're going to be in the future. As we've said, during your fifties, there is still enough runway left to achieve a successful takeoff, no matter how many challenges you're facing today.

Chances are, you've already made some progress, but you might not yet clearly understand how your current financial situation relates to your goals. By taking a thorough inventory of your financial health, you can figure out exactly where you stand on the path to your destination.

Most people just have a vague or general idea of what they have, how it works, and what it all means.

Clarifying your current financial status is a bit like dumping all the pieces of a puzzle onto a table, flipping them over, and sorting them out. From there, you have to figure out how to put together all of those pieces to create the big picture so you can look at it and say, "Okay, this is what we have, and this is where we are." Much like an x-ray or MRI machine gets to the current truth in the health world, this process provides you with much-needed clarity on where things stand financially.

First, gather up all of your important financial documents—anything that a dollar touches—like your will, personal tax returns, 401(k) and investment statements, annuities, and life insurance policies. If you have employee benefits at work, like a pension or health, disability, or group life insurance, you might find all of that in your employee manual.

You'll need to pull together all of your bank accounts, credit card statements, and mortgage statements for any properties you have financed. If you're in business, you might also include employee agreements, business tax returns, and any stock options, if applicable. Basically, you want to catalog the value of all of your assets and liabilities. Whenever we meet with people for the first time, we tell them they are like a blank white piece of canvas to us, and we need to paint in the picture with all of these details.

Then, you'll want to clarify your cash flow resources and needs. Exactly how much money is coming in from all sources and how much is going out every month? What sources of income do you anticipate in the future, such as Social Security or pension payments from current or former employers. If you have inherited a retirement account from a parent, you may have required minimum distributions to take out each year.

This probably doesn't sound like a fun activity, but it is essential to good financial planning. You have to know exactly what you're dealing with in order to make accurate projections about what you'll have available to you in the future and what gaps there may be to fill along the way.

More than likely, you will be energized by this process as you begin to feel organized and empowered about the wise decisions you have made and the assets you have accumulated thus far. Even some people who have not been paying close attention to these things are surprised to find that they are often in better shape than they realized.

But, we also understand that this part of the process can be incredibly discouraging to some people. Your picture might reveal that you're a lot further from your retirement goals than you thought. Don't beat yourself up over it. Know this for sure: there are people in better shape than you and people who have been in much worse financial condition than you who still managed to retire successfully. Just by tallying things up today, you've started making progress toward where you want to be.

Plus, let's face it, this is *your* life, not someone else's. You can't use someone else's plan to build your goals. It's easy to start comparing yourself to others and feeling bad that you haven't made more progress, but this isn't a competition. It doesn't matter what the studies and statistics say about where people your age *should* be. Don't fall into that trap! You are playing your own game, and it will be different than just about everyone else's for a reason.

Whether you are looking at the statistics and saying, "I'm way behind where I should be" or saying, "I'm ahead of everyone else. I'm doing great," both mindsets are misguided. In reality, how you're doing compared to other people at the same stage in life doesn't tell you whether or not you're in good shape.

You're in good shape if you're on track toward your own retirement goals. That's it. That's the measuring stick. But since most people don't actually have financial goals to begin with to measure against, it's impossible to tell what kind of shape they are in. It's *not knowing* more than anything else that is the source of most of the worry, anxiety, and confusion about retirement.

Most people don't truly know where they currently stand on basic things like account balances, asset allocation, details of group benefits, and other financial details. The main question we want you to answer affirmatively is, "Do you know?" By painting in the big picture of where you currently stand with your finances, you gain tremendous power to shape and adjust your financial future. Now you know what all of the pieces are and what they do, so you can sit down and talk to your spouse, your kids, trusted friends, or a financial advisor, and start moving in the right direction with confidence.

THE ONLY THING THAT MATTERS

It's easy to get confused by all of the noise that you're subjected to 24/7. How do the daily movements of the stock market impact your progress toward your retirement goals? Are your investments keeping up with the market or the brother-in-law or guy at work who is constantly bragging about his wins? If the Dow Jones drops 200 points, should you worry? If the federal government passes more changes to the tax laws, does it change your big picture? What will this year's annual "end of the

For help getting your current finances in order, download our free Runway Decade Strategic Organizer at *www.runwaydecade. com*. With this tool, you'll be able to identify all of the elements of your financial health and start making progress toward your long-term financial goals. The organizer includes a checklist, an income/expense template, and a way to list all investments, insurance, bank statements, real estate details, mortgages, values, interest rates, and more.

financial world" message be, and should you adjust your plan accordingly?

People who get caught up in the headlines can lose clarity and a sense of direction about their financial progress and cause themselves some sleepless nights. The main thing you need to be focusing on is where you stand in relation to your long-term financial goals, and in many cases, it should be the only thing you pay attention to. It's the main thing that gives people confidence about the future, especially if they realize they have a little buffer. Creating that margin of safety like we discussed earlier is crucial to weathering any short-term problems or market events, but don't ever take your eyes off the prize.

Getting organized is the most helpful thing you can do for yourself. If you know where you want to go, and you know where you are now, then you can move forward with a sense of confidence, despite all of the noise. With big-picture clarity, you now have the power to press the accelerator knowing for sure that you're headed in the right direction.

To use our opening metaphor, you now know exactly where Space Mountain is, and you know exactly where you are in the park in relation to Space Mountain. Your next step is to trace a path from here to there and make sure that you can reach the destination in the limited time that's available to you. To do that, you'll factor in all of the twists and turns along the way, note any obstacles or difficulties you might encounter, and select what appears to be the best and safest route. Some of these we detailed in the previous chapter.

But if you break your leg on the way to Space Mountain because you took a risky shortcut, no one's going to be able to enjoy the ride because you won't even get there, in which case, what was the point of all of that hard work and sacrifice?

The same goes for your retirement. The best path forward will help you accumulate the money you need to live the retirement lifestyle you've envisioned, but a successful retirement is about more than money. It's also about your overall wellness. You want to make sure that when you get to the finish line, you'll be able to enjoy a happy, *healthy* retirement, because there are some things money can't fix.

ARE YOU EVEN GOING TO GET THERE?

"When health is absent, wisdom cannot reveal itself,
art cannot manifest, strength cannot fight, wealth
becomes useless, and intelligence cannot be applied."
—Herophilus, ancient Greek physician

O ur friend Dr. Curtis Chastain runs a concierge medical practice at Our Lady of the Lake Hospital in Baton Rouge, Louisiana. There is a story that he tells about part of what motivated him to start the Lake Men's

Health Center and Executive Wellness Program. It goes like this:

A woman's husband collapsed suddenly after dinner one evening, so she called 911. He was rushed to the hospital and taken to the ICU. As the medical team fought to save his life, his distraught wife sat in the waiting room, anxiously waiting for some kind of update about his condition.

Finally, Dr. Chastain stepped into the waiting room to speak to her, and she rushed to meet him.

"What's wrong with him, Doctor? Is he going to be alright?" she asked.

"I'm afraid your husband has had a heart attack," Dr. Chastain explained.

The woman gasped, her eyes widening. "A heart attack? I can't believe it. How did this happen?"

He tried to comfort her with his best bedside manner. "Well, bad things happen to good people, and the body just wears out over time, but we're doing everything we can to help him." But that's not exactly what he was thinking.

"What do you mean, 'How did this happen?'" he thought to himself. "His heart attack didn't *just happen*. It was simply the final blow of a growing health crisis that he'd been steadily marching toward since age twenty-five. And now at sixty, after many years of a bad diet, lack of exercise, and too much stress, it was too late to avoid the inevitable."

Of course, he didn't say this to the woman's face at the time, but that brief conversation in the waiting room changed the course of his career. He realized that it wasn't enough to treat people *after* a health crisis. Somehow, he had to intervene earlier and help people find ways to change their lifestyles so they could live longer, healthier, happier lives.

Going into retirement in great financial shape *and* great physical shape goes hand-in-hand with helping you live your ideal vision of the future. That's why you're reading a chapter about health in a book about establishing your pre-retirement plan in your fifties. The two disciplines are related in many ways. Notably, if you sacrifice your health to build wealth, you will eventually sacrifice your wealth trying to restore your health.

But the parallels don't stop there.

THE INTERSECTION OF HEALTH AND WEALTH

Studies have shown that money is the number one cause of stress for many Americans, and worrying about money has been linked with poor physical and emotional health. We talked earlier about the stress of being disorganized, drifting forward without a plan, and not knowing where you stand in relation to your goals. Could that same stress also manifest itself as poorer health, further compounding the problem?

Both financially successful people and healthy people tend to have a propensity toward planning. In the financial sense, this skillset allows you to delay the gratification of spending everything so you can store up those unspent resources to enjoy more freedom later. From a health standpoint, it means passing on the immediate gratification of unhealthy foods or long periods of inactivity now so you can enjoy a healthier lifestyle. That same ability to proactively plan is also what leads you to seek out professional medical or financial advice.

It turns out that the do-it-yourself crowd is equally small in both areas. Very few people are able to implement great health *and* wealth habits on their own without some form of outside accountability. Achieving and maintaining good health and wealth both require discipline, and that's a problem for most people. In both worlds, physicians and financial advisors advocate breaking down large tasks like losing weight, getting fit, lowering cholesterol, and saving for retirement or college into small steps and daily habits.

While surprises exist in both areas that can seemingly hit from out of nowhere, many negative health and wealth outcomes are preventable, or at least containable, with proactive awareness, education, and planning. Both areas benefit from setting realistic goals and measuring those goals against certain benchmarks and mile markers periodically to remain on track.

These disciplines and habits also have a long-term positive compounding effect over time, spilling over into many other areas of your life, such as mental health, relationships, and career satisfaction.

We could go on, but suffice it to say, there are many parallels between health and wealth, and chief among them is the positive effect of early detection.

STEPPING OVER THE SNAKE

With regard to health, the sooner a doctor knows about a condition like cancer or heart disease, the better chance they have to guide you to the help you need to change the course you're on. Early detection is the key to fixing something that's not quite right before it's too late. Dr. Chastain calls this "stepping over the snake."

Knowing your family's medical history is one good way to get out in front of some of the big snakes that can sneak up and bite you. Cancer, heart disease, high blood pressure, high cholesterol, and many other health problems have genetic factors. If you know which of these you may be predisposed to, you can be on the lookout for them with your doctor's help. Catching them in the early stages of development is critical.

Actually, early detection is the key to both health *and* wealth, and good health is just as important as having enough money to retire. In fact, uncovered healthcare expenses are the leading cause of bankruptcy during retirement, and they are also among the highest rising consumer costs annually.

If you are among the healthy and fortunate, you probably don't have a lot of medical expenses yet. However, by the time you get to the end of the pre-retirement runway, even more so in your seventies and eighties, you will most likely be on a number of medications, have regular doctor appointments, and even have the occasional hospital visit.

By then, these bodies of ours start breaking down, and it can take a whole lot of medical care to keep them going. At age sixty-five, the lifetime likelihood of needing significant long-term care (defined as requiring help with two or more activities of daily living) is 75 percent for women and 64 percent for men.[3] Even with Medicare kicking in after age

---

3   Richard W. Johnson, Urban Institute, "What Is the Lifetime Risk of Needing and Receiving Long-Term Services and Supports?," prepared under contract with the US Department of Health and Human Services, April 3, 2019, https://aspe.hhs.gov/reports/what-lifetime-risk-needing-receiving-long-term-services-supports.

sixty-five, there can be significant expenses related to your healthcare that are not fully covered, such as home health or assisted living, so if you aren't prepared to absorb the cost, the impact might be disastrous.

The idea is to head as much of this off at the pass as you can by being proactive. If there is a natural curve to aging and physical decline, your mission is to bend that curve outward as much as possible by ramping up your positive health habits while you are in the runway decade. The results will not only be seen in your health, but in your wallet as well.

According to HealthView Services' *2021 Retirement Healthcare Costs Data Report*, the total projected lifetime healthcare costs for a healthy sixty-five-year-old couple retiring in 2021 are expected to be $662,156. And it's only going to get more expensive. Healthcare costs are expected to continue their historical trend of rising at a rate of 2 to 2.5 times that of US inflation.[4]

You will do yourself a huge favor if you can enter retirement without debt *and* in good health. Having plenty of money doesn't mean much if you can't enjoy it, and you certainly won't benefit from being the "richest person in the graveyard"! While health problems and death are

---

4   HealthView Services, *2021 Retirement Healthcare Costs Data Report*, https://hvsfinancial.com/wp-content/uploads/2020/12/2021-Retirement-Healthcare-Costs-Data-Report.pdf.

inevitable, there's a direct link between health and stress. As we said, money matters, especially debt, are among the most stressful when you're living on a fixed income. If you can reduce your own stress by establishing some healthy habits now, both physically *and* financially, your body will benefit and reward you as you age.

If you haven't already done so, your fifties are the perfect decade for setting up healthy habits to carry with you into retirement. This is the time to become proactive, and it starts with getting annual checkups. Sadly, according to a survey from the Cleveland Clinic, only three in five men get an annual physical, and only a little more than 40 percent seek medical attention when they fear they have a serious medical condition. In fact, the survey reveals that 72 percent of men surveyed "would rather do household chores than go to the doctor." That means they would rather step over a literal snake doing yard work than they would a figurative one with their health!

The key is to get a full physical evaluation of where you are now to establish a baseline, set some goals on the quality of life you want to live, and then get regular checkups to keep your finger on the pulse of how you are progressing or if any changes need to be made along the way.

Isn't it interesting how much that sounds like financial planning?

If you get to age sixty and haven't prepared well for retirement, then unless you receive an inheritance or windfall of some kind, it's too late. At that point, you have limited options, including a drastically reduced lifestyle, continuing to work as long as your body holds up, or taking the dreaded drive across town to ask your kids for help. It's like the woman in the waiting room asking, "How did this happen?" It didn't just happen, of course, because like your health, saving, investing, and planning are all disciplines.

Showing up at retirement without adequate resources is like showing up at the emergency room during a heart attack. As painful as the truth is sometimes, the time to detect and fix the problem was years ago while you were still on the runway.

Stepping over the snake applies to your finances as much as it does to your health, especially as your resources grow. We spoke to a client who had built up substantial assets over his long career so that he was worth $5 million as he entered the runway decade. Because of his financial success, he was approached by a friend with an opportunity to make a big investment in a startup. The kicker was that besides a cash contribution, he had to personally guarantee his share of a loan the company needed for funding, which was about $2 million. If the project went sideways, he was on the hook for the downside.

After analyzing the risk and reward of this investment opportunity with him, we pointed out that the amount he stood to lose if the project failed would negatively impact his lifestyle decisions and future much more than any potential gain would enhance his future.

"You've spent your entire career building up this $5 million," we said. "Do you really want to risk so much of it on a single bet, when you could lose $2 million overnight? You're already going to have enough to fund your plans. Do you really need to double down to try and have way more than enough?"

It was enough perspective and information for him to decide to turn down the opportunity. Ultimately, he stepped over the snake on that one. Sure, it might have worked out in his favor if he'd invested in it, but it simply wasn't worth the risk at that point in his life, especially after he'd done so many things right.

Of course, we're not health, fitness, or nutrition experts (although we like to joke that we did stay at a Holiday Inn Express last night!). Those are not our lanes, so we encourage you to turn to people who can speak more specifically about healthier habits and making smart health choices. We are experienced enough to know that retirement success has both a financial and a physical component. You have to spend time taking care of both, because each will

ON A PERSONAL NOTE:
BILL'S FIFTIETH BIRTHDAY SURPRISE

I first noticed the dull pain in my right upper arm a mere four days after my fiftieth birthday. I was loading the last pieces of furniture onto a trailer with my nephew in the sweltering Louisiana August heat. It was the final load of a move to Baton Rouge. Along with the sudden arm pain, I started seeing stars. In my mind, I chalked it up to the brutal heat and maybe a pulled muscle. We took a needed break, finished loading, and hit the road.

Over the course of the next few weeks, I noticed the arm pain popping up again three or four times while on long walks or exercising. By this time it was becoming clear to me that the arm pain was connected to physical exertion. I really wanted to believe it was nothing major. After all, I was healthy, a nonsmoker, diet-conscious, fairly young, and I had always been told that I was the "healthiest" one in the family.

Still, rather than becoming one of those guys who says, "It's nothing," and ignores the symptoms, I decided I should track down the cause. Unfortunately, I was living in a new city with no doctor. One morning, after feeling arm pain just by taking out the garbage, I drove myself to the nearest emergency room. From there, I had an appointment with a cardiologist, a battery of tests, and ultimately a date with the cath lab. Welcome to fifty!

continued...

In framing up my expectations for the heart cath, cardiologist Dr. Davey Prout prepared me for all the possible outcomes: stroke, heart attack, stents, bypass surgery. The night before the procedure, I couldn't help but think of some of the worst-case scenarios and what they would mean for my family. Had I done enough to ensure that they would be okay? What if I had a heart attack right there on the table and didn't make it?

I felt woefully unprepared.

During the procedure, Dr. Prout discovered that I had 100 percent blockage in one of the branches of a major artery (the LAD). He performed a balloon angioplasty and inserted a stent. The doctor later told me that even though there was no evidence I'd had a heart attack, I was a prime candidate for one if I had waited much longer. And, as he made clear, heart attacks involving the LAD often don't have the best outcome.

Seemingly out of nowhere, this episode had me staring my own mortality in the face. Was fifty years of life all I was going to get? Fortunately, because I was able to catch it early enough, the stent not only saved my life, but it also opened my eyes.

Lifestyle changes would have to be made, for sure. Before I turned fifty, I was never prescribed a daily medication. Now, I'm on several, but I'm still here! Had I not been paying attention to my own health, I might not have realized I had a problem until it was too late.

most certainly impact the other. Think of health and wealth as dance partners, always needing to move in rhythm.

In the simplest terms, one of two things will happen in your lifetime: either your money will outlive you, or you will outlive your money. Even though they are dance partners, only one of those outcomes is good, and it's the only one worth striving for while there is time left on the clock.

But you don't want to outlive your money because you left the planet too soon. Ideally, you and your money will enjoy a long and fruitful partnership, and it will outlive you to benefit those you will ultimately leave behind in the world.

Our goal in addressing your health here is that you will simply keep this top of mind right alongside your financial considerations for retirement. What a shame it would be to plan for a great retirement only to miss out on it because bad health habits cut your life short. Unfortunately, it's safe to say we can all think of people in our lives, maybe a friend, family member, or classmate, who didn't make it to retirement because of bad health. Or maybe they made it, but then they didn't last long enough to truly enjoy it.

Obviously, there are no guarantees in life, and even people who make smart choices can still find themselves in an unexpected health crisis. Bill's best childhood friend, Steve, developed a rare brain tumor and died shortly after turning fifty. Similarly, one of Pete's middle school teammates, Wally, barely made it to his mid-fifties. Both of those guys were otherwise healthy prior to their diagnoses, and both had every reason to believe they would live a long and healthy life. But life dealt them another card that was out of their control.

Outside of being dealt a bad card, we just have to do what we can and take action where needed. As Bill's story illustrates, it's smart to pay attention to the warning signs your body is giving you and take action accordingly. Like most things, we have little control over the outcomes, but a lot of control over the inputs. You can certainly fine-tune your choices and habits to reduce that dreadful and ever-present "margin of error," and at the very least, you can increase your odds of living a longer, healthier, wealthier, and happier life. As the ancient poet Virgil said, "The greatest wealth is health."

Or Augusten Burroughs said, "When you have your health, you have everything. When you do not have your health, nothing else matters at all." We certainly agree with that in theory, but, assuming you have your health and are steadily progressing down the runway, there's a whole lot more that matters. There are many dials and gauges on the retirement dashboard, and it's important to review everything a dollar touches as you set yourself up for a great flight plan and final approach.

LISTEN TO THE HEALTH EXPERTS

We are not health, nutrition, or fitness experts, so here are some resources from experts who can help you introduce healthy habits into your life. It's not too late to make changes that will impact your longevity and well-being as you approach retirement.

- American Heart Association (AHA): *www.heart.org*
- American Cancer Society: *www.cancer.org*
- AARP: *www.aarp.org*
- *The Obesity Code* by Dr. Jason Fung
- *Younger Next Year* by Chris Crowley and Henry S. Lodge, M.D.

ENTER THE MATRIX

"To know what you know and what you
do not know, that is true knowledge."
—Confucius, Ancient Chinese philosopher

f you're like most people, when you hear or think of
the terms "financial advice" or "financial advisor," your
mind goes straight to investments and investing. Indeed,
investments *do* play a huge role and are a major spoke
in the wheel of a well-rounded approach to managing
your overall financial life. They will usually pay for a lot in
retirement, but when you think of wealth management or

holistic financial planning, there are so many other spokes in the wheel that have to be tended to. As you make your pre-retirement plan, you'll want to look at and monitor anything that a dollar touches in your life.

If you have ever seen the cockpit dashboard of an airplane, it can seem overwhelming and intimidating. There are gauges and dials of all shapes and sizes all over the place. So many, in fact, that you might wonder how the pilot and co-pilot can keep up with them all. The truth is, there are just a handful that they pay attention to most of the time. The others are there for more details if one of the main dials indicates a problem. Also, some are big-picture dials, while others are specific indicator gauges.

Envision your overall financial life in a similar layout.

When you think of retirement, you probably tend to think about things like your IRA, 401(k), pension plan, and Social Security, but it might be more accurate to think of retirement planning as one of the big dials in your financial life, with other specific financial components as small gauges underneath. As you set yourself up for a successful takeoff, it's important to consider what every dial or gauge on your control panel is doing, not just for the retirement dial but all the other main dials as well.

As you visualize your dashboard and think about your ideal vision of the future, imagine that there are seven specific large dials across the top with the following headings:

- Cash flow and budgeting
- Investment planning
- Retirement planning
- Income tax planning
- Risk management and insurance
- Estate planning and charitable giving
- Assistance to others

While a financial plan is always very personal to the individual, these seven categories apply in some way to most people. And just like on a real pilot dashboard, each of these has a host of related sub-gauges that go along with them. Make sure you're paying attention to all of them as you start to make your way down the runway toward retirement.

It's impossible to put every nuance that might come up on a sheet of paper, but we've designed an easy-to-follow Financial Matrix that can help you get started looking at the main categories and asking yourself the right questions. Begin with the question, "Do you know?" If you're not 100 percent sure you're in good shape in any particular area, then it's best to admit you don't know so you can seek out a solution.

The matrix is not an all-encompassing list, but it's a reasonable place to start. Often, when people see it for the first time, it jogs their memory about something they've needed clarity on, or reminds them of a solution to something they've been putting off. Take a look at the matrix here and highlight or note any areas that need attention in your situation. We'll go into each of them in a little more detail.

You can also download your own copy at *www.runway decade.com.*

CASH FLOW AND BUDGETING

We touched on this briefly earlier in the book when we suggested that you know your numbers, specifically through the use of an Income Statement. There are all kinds of great apps and tech tools to help you budget and track your money in and money out, and the best one is the one that you will actually use. How you direct and manage your cash flow has implications all over the matrix, especially retirement planning.

How much income will you need in order to live comfortably throughout your retirement? Some experts suggest it's around 75 to 80 percent of your working years' income. Which expenses will fall out, and which are going to stick around? Which expenses will go up, and which may go

YOUR FINANCIAL MATRIX

INCOME TAX PLANNING
- Review of Cost-Basis
- Review Realized Gains
- Carry Forward Losses
- Tax Loss Harvesting
- Deductions and Credits
- Health Savings and Flexible Spending Accounts

CASH FLOW AND BUDGET
- Income Sources
- Expenses and Budgeting
- Debt Management
- One-Time Expenses
- Planned Large Expenses
- Emercency Funding
- Mortgage Review
- Lines of Credit

RISK MANAGEMENT AND INSURANCE
- Review of Existing Policies
- Life Insurance Needs
- Long Term Care Insurance
- Disability Insurance
- Health Insurance
- Homeowner's or Renter's Insurance
- Liability Coverage

INVESTMENT PLANNING
- Portfolio Analysis
- Asset Allocation
- Risk Tolerance and Time Horizon
- Income Strategies
- Investment Policy Statement
- Taxable vs. Tax Deferred
- Fee Cost Analysis

ESTATE PLANNING AND CHARITABLE GIVING
- Wills
- Power of Attorney
- Living Will
- Health Care Proxy
- Trust
- Irrevocable Life Insurance Trusts
- Estate Taxes
- Guardians for Minor Children
- Charitable Giving and Trusts

RETIREMENT PLANNING
- Withdrawal Strategies
- Social Security and Medicare
- Business Exit Planning
- IRA Contributions and Conversions
- Employer-Sponsored Plans and 401(k)s
- Annuities and Pensions
- Retirement Income Projections
- Self-Employed Retirement Plans

ASSISTANCE TO OTHERS
- Gifting
- Education Planning
- Caring for Elderly
- 529 College Savings Plans
- Roth IRAs for Children
- UGMA/UTMA

down? Typically, you need less income in retirement because you are no longer funding your 401(k) each month, and hopefully your mortgage and other debts are paid off. The amount you spend on healthcare will almost certainly increase, but how much is hard to tell and will involve a lot of factors. Will you be spending more on traveling and going out in the early years of retirement? It's always a good exercise to stop at least once per year and think about the things that will impact your cash flow and budgeting.

While you are on the runway, this column is where you allocate funds to your specific goals, like building your emergency cash reserves, paying down your debts, and investing for retirement and wealth building. While your income sources might come mainly from earned income at this stage of life, eventually some of those subcategories under the Retirement Planning column will replace income from a job if you are able to fund them properly.

Among your objectives, when looking at your cash flow and budgeting, is to determine if there is money leaking out in the form of paying higher interest charges on mortgage debt or lines of credit. Are there opportunities to refinance, consolidate, or otherwise reduce your interest expense so you can accelerate the payoffs?

Last, for your liquid cash savings and money market funds, make sure you are earning the highest FDIC-covered rates available. Many banks and brokerages pay a fraction of the interest that can be found with reputable institutions offering high interest accounts online. The bigger your balances, the more "lost" interest is leaking out that can be used to bolster cash reserves, increase retirement investments, purchase long-term care insurance, or fund some other important goal.

INVESTMENT PLANNING

Many people are on cruise control when it comes to their investments, but it's important to keep an eye on what your money is doing. Portfolios can get out of balance for many good reasons, including certain parts of them performing better relative to others. As markets go up and down, the holdings in your account will change in value, but not equally. As that happens over time, the asset allocation and risk profile of the portfolio change along with it.

It is estimated that over 50 million Americans actively participate in a 401(k) plan where they work, but according to a 2014 study by Aon Hewitt, only 19 percent of employees in plans they studied had rebalanced their accounts that year.[5] Rebalancing is the process of bringing the percent-

---

5   AON, "Despite Record-High 401(k) Plan Balances, Few Workers...

age allocation of the funds in your account back to their originally desired investment style, objective, or risk tolerance. If you never rebalance, the funds or holdings in your account will eventually not reflect your original wishes or ideas, and by not paying attention, you will have given up control as to how it is invested.

This is often true as people change jobs and leave old retirement accounts behind in their former employers' plans, where they are out of sight, out of mind. These orphaned accounts are almost always portable and can be transferred into your new employer's plan or rolled into a personal IRA, where they can be periodically adjusted as the allocation changes due to market fluctuations.

We met with a guy in his early seventies not long ago whose investment portfolio was very aggressive for his age and stage of life, and he didn't even know it. When he reached out to us to look into his portfolio and discuss retirement, he discovered that he'd done much better than he expected, mainly because his allocation had become more and more aggressive over time, and it had worked in his favor. But when we showed him the maximum decline

...Are Actively Managing Their Portfolios," May 28, 2015, https://ir.aon.com/about-aon/investor-relations/investor-news/news-release-details/2015/Despite-Record-High-401k-Plan-Balances-Few-Workers-are-Actively-Managing-their-Portfolios/default.aspx.

a portfolio of that mix would have experienced in past market corrections, he was eager to rebalance to diversify his risk heading into retirement.

While it's not good to make reactive decisions to short-term market corrections, it is important to make sure your investments line up with your financial goals, your risk tolerance, and your time horizon. It pays to be proactive, rebalancing into the strength of market advances while avoiding the panic of market pullbacks.

It's also imperative to consider the tax ramifications of the many different types of investments that are available to you. Most types of retirement accounts, like 401(k)s, IRAs, and annuities, grow tax-deferred until the funds are withdrawn, but you have limited access to them because of early withdrawal penalties from the IRS if taken before age fifty-nine-and-a-half.

When you "double-click" on the Investment Planning column, the main drop-down bullet or subcategory to focus on is the investment policy statement. This document spells out the goals and strategy for the particular investment portfolio in question and can always be referred to when making allocation or rebalancing decisions. Every portfolio should be invested toward a specific goal you have (e.g., retirement, college education, legacy building) and not simply invested to beat the market, which in and of itself doesn't tell you if you'll have enough. Beating the market is not a financial goal. It's important to know the purpose the portfolio is put in service to achieve.

Keeping a balance between personal, taxable investments and tax-deferred retirement investments as you approach the end of the runway can give you more options as you make decisions as to the timing of your ultimate retirement date.

RETIREMENT PLANNING

When it comes to retirement planning, while you are still on the runway, perhaps the biggest question is about whether you have run detailed retirement income projections to get your arms around where you currently stand. This will give you a sense of how much your accounts may be worth at certain ages with your current funding level and identify any potential gaps you may need to make up while there is still time.

Taking full advantage of the tax-deferred compounding benefits of IRAs, 401(k)s, profit-sharing plans, pension plans, and annuities can serve to accelerate your progress toward your retirement goal.

If you are self-employed or own a business, you have a maze of options to consider for establishing your own retirement plan, some of which, like cash balance plans, allow you to contribute substantially more than others each year. Also, your business exit strategy will come into play, as the value of the business is often a business owner's largest asset.

Besides your retirement account values, have you identified all of the other financial pieces that are going to play a role in your retirement? For example, do you know how things like Social Security, pensions, and, if applicable, your spouse's retirement benefits will factor into your retirement income? You don't need to make decisions today about when to take your Social Security, but you definitely should go to their website at *www.ssa.gov* and get an idea of your monthly benefits at different ages (e.g., sixty-two, sixty-seven, seventy). Your puzzle pieces will be different from anyone else's, so it's important at this stage to lay them all on the table, flip them over, and start framing the edges of the retirement income puzzle.

Remember, Medicare doesn't start until age sixty-five, so if you're planning to retire at sixty-two, you will need a plan to cover your own healthcare expenses for a few years. Over the years, fewer and fewer employers are paying for retiree healthcare benefits, so that might be a significant expense to prepare for if you plan to stop working before you are eligible for Medicare.

If you are closer to the end of the runway than the beginning, you'll also need to start thinking about your withdrawal strategy. This gets to the specific order of the accounts you will draw income from and the amount from each. You don't have to make a concrete decision about this now, but it needs to be on your mind so you can position the accounts for the withdrawal phase rather than the accumulation phase they have been in thus far. Just having a bunch of money in various accounts doesn't automatically make this an easy issue because there's usually a best tax-efficient strategy to employ to meet your income needs.

We spoke to a prospective client who had in excess of $8 million scattered among multiple taxable and tax-deferred accounts, but he was struggling to figure out how to turn that money into a regular income stream.

"Do I just take money out of my savings account every week to replace my paycheck, or should I be primarily using interest and dividend disbursements from my investments and holding on to the savings?"

This is a common conversation. Even if you have accumulated substantial assets, it's still not a simple or straightforward decision. Which accounts should be relied on for current income, and which ones are better for future income? We'll talk a bit more about this in Chapter 7.

INCOME TAX PLANNING

In client discussions over many years, hardly anything irritates people as much as paying too much in unnecessary taxes. It's kind of humorous actually, but if given the choice between making an extra dollar or saving a dollar in taxes, most people will pick the latter every single time! Both put one extra dollar in your pocket, but for people who earn a high income and already pay a lot toward a host of different taxes, saving a tax dollar just feels better.

We talked about money leaking out earlier; one of the best ways to stop leaks is to make sure you're not overpaying on your income taxes between now and retirement. We're not talking about tax *evasion*, which means not paying taxes you legally owe (and is highly illegal). We're talking about tax *avoidance*, which is the act of arranging your financial matters in such a way as to *not* pay what you *don't* legally have to pay. In fact, you have no obligation whatsoever to pay more than you owe, yet many people do so unaware.

In the 1934 case *Helvering v. Gregory*, Federal Appellate Judge Learned Hand ruled, "Any one may so arrange his affairs so that his taxes shall be as low as possible; he is not bound to choose that pattern which best pays the

Treasury; there is not even a patriotic duty to increase one's taxes."[6]

For example, municipal bond interest is free from federal taxes and usually free from state income taxes of the issuing state or municipality. If you put money into a Roth IRA, you can avoid paying taxes on what the account earns along the way, and even when you pull it out at retirement. You can buy an annuity, which grows tax-deferred until it is withdrawn, giving you control of when you pay the tax on its earnings. Or you can put money in a standard 401(k) and get a tax deduction now and watch it grow tax-deferred until you withdraw it. All of these can reduce your current year's tax bill.

Proactively offsetting capital gains and losses each year before the clock strikes midnight on December 31st is a process referred to as "loss harvesting." This is a strategy to reduce the amount of capital gains taxes you will pay when you file your tax return for that year. Since you are taxed on the net sum of your gains, it makes sense to lower the amount of gains you will have in order to reduce your

---

6   Helvering v. Gregory, 69 F.2d 809, 810 (2d Cir. 1934), quoted in Christopher Bergin, "Tax Avoidance Just Isn't What It Used To Be," Forbes, September 17, 2013, https://www.forbes.com/sites/taxanalysts/2013/09/17/tax-avoidance-just-isnt-what-it-used-to-be/?sh=550fad7d5747.

tax bill. However, if those transactions don't occur before the end of the tax year, the opportunity is lost forever. Any extra dollar you pay in taxes is a dollar you no longer have in your financial picture to use elsewhere.

There are also plenty of legal tax deductions and credits that taxpayers leave on the table each year. Making sure you take full advantage of them is always a good idea. By eliminating any excess income taxes, you'll have more money to invest or to fund other goals as you approach retirement.

While we aren't CPAs or accountants, when we meet with clients, we typically ask to look at the previous two years of income tax returns so we can make sure they're not paying more than they should. We've found some significant tax errors in our careers that would have gone unnoticed until it was too late to do anything about them. Often, if you catch a mistake in time, it's possible to amend your tax return and get some or all of it back. Imagine finding out that you overpaid by $10,000 or $20,000 or more. We've seen it happen firsthand, and had it not been caught, that money would have disappeared into the black hole of the IRS forever instead of staying in the client accounts where it rightfully belonged.

Don't feel embarrassed by income tax mistakes—the tax code is absurdly complex, and mistakes are all too common—but it's also one of the ultimate "Do you know?" questions. Do you really know if you're sending the IRS more money than you have to, and if not, what can you do to find out?

RISK MANAGEMENT AND INSURANCE

When building a solid financial plan for the future, planning for all the things that can go *right* with your plan is a luxury you have after you've planned for all the things that can go *wrong*. When we ponder the various risks we have, it's all about the things we can lose, sometimes without a moment's notice: your life, your health, your ability to earn an income, your home, your other assets, and so on.

There's no sense avoiding the harsh truth. Despite saving a lot of money, there are some things that can wipe you out financially, or at least significantly impact your family's ability to stay in their world, financially speaking— especially if you don't wake up tomorrow, or you're unable to go to work. To avoid this, you need to have some plans in place for assessing and managing the impact of these known risks. Many people despise paying for insurance, but it's a smart way to share some of these big risks with an insurance company so you don't have to bear the full brunt of the burden should you suffer one of these losses.

Former US Supreme Court Justice Louis D. Brandeis once wrote[7,8]:

"I live in Alexandria, Virginia. Near the Supreme Court chambers is a toll bridge across the Potomac. When in a rush, I pay the dollar toll and get home early. However, I usually drive outside the downtown section of the city and cross the Potomac on

a free bridge. This bridge was placed outside the downtown Washington, D.C. area to serve a useful social service: getting drivers to drive the extra mile to alleviate congestion during rush hour. If I went over the toll bridge and through the barrier without paying the toll, I would be committing tax evasion.

continued...

7   Supreme Court Justice Louis D. Brandeis (1856-1941), in his essay entitled *Thoughts on Legitimate Tax Avoidance*.

8   Image: Harris & Ewing, *Louis Brandeis, 1916, Creative Commons License*.

...continued

If, however, I drive the extra mile outside the city of Washington and take the free bridge, I am using a legitimate, logical, and suitable method of tax avoidance, and I am performing a useful social service by doing so. For my tax evasion, I should be punished. For my tax avoidance, I should be commended. The tragedy of life is that so few people know that the free bridge even exists! There are free bridges located within the Internal Revenue Code which allow you to legitimately avoid unnecessary taxes...the key is to know where to find them. Becoming informed is not enough—once informed, you need to take action—informed people who don't act lose just as much as uninformed people who can't act."

Legal and ethical tax avoidance helps you build wealth along the runway.

Of course, you hope and expect that your retirement plan will come together and everything will work out perfectly, but it's wise to have a plan if it doesn't. What if you experience a major unexpected health crisis with large out-of-pocket expenses? What would your scenario look like if you suddenly couldn't work for years before retirement or if you needed around-the-clock medical care? What would happen to your family if you or your spouse has suddenly seen your last sunrise? If your house burns down, is hit by a hurricane or tornado, or floods, will you have the money to repair it?

In all of these instances, the great plans you've made and the wealth you've so carefully accumulated could be at risk. Have you stopped to consider all of the downside risks you have? Do you have plans in place to mitigate and manage these risks? That usually comes down to some form of being well-insured in these critical areas. Like other areas of the matrix, it comes down to the question, "Do you know?"

On the other end of the spectrum, we meet some people who are over-insured or, as one person put it, "insurance poor" from all the excess premiums they are paying. They're on cruise control, paying for policies they will never need, because they've either gotten bad advice along the way or outgrew the original purpose of the coverage.

Sometimes this takes the form of duplicate coverage, where they have money leaking out with multiple policies protecting the same thing.

We met someone who had three different types of disability coverage, which he initially thought were stacked on top of one another for benefit purposes. When we asked him why he structured it this way, he said, "Well, this one pays $10,000. This one pays $5,000. And this third one will pay $2,500 per month for a total of $17,500 per month."

What he didn't realize is that his policies had different payment priorities built into their contract language that stipulated they would only pay out once other coverages stopped. In other words, he wasn't going to get all three payouts. He would only get one for sure, and he might never get the other two, thus paying for something that would have very likely turned out to be nothing.

Think about all of the money he had poured into premiums that he could have invested or used for another goal. This is by no means an isolated incident. It happens all too often, particularly with old permanent life insurance policies that are no longer needed. People typically don't *buy* financial products like that, they get *sold* financial products like that. And the person doing the selling may not have the client's best interests at heart, or may not be incentivized to explain all of the nuances of a new insurance policy, especially how it might interact with someone's other existing policies.

Even when they are competent, very few insurance professionals are thinking holistically about the entire wealth picture. Most of them are product salespeople who sit in specific lanes with a narrow body of knowledge, so they aren't equipped to provide a comprehensive overview of how their recommendations will intersect with the rest of your finances.

The best way to know where you stand in managing these various risk areas is to first determine your needs, fully audit your existing coverage, and then seek out the solutions to fill any gaps that may exist. Because insurance premiums can be pricey and are always changing in the marketplace, this can be a good area to look for more money leaking out.

ESTATE PLANNING AND CHARITABLE GIVING

Let's face it, none of us are getting out of here alive. In fact, since you never know when the last grain of sand is going to drop through the hourglass of life, there will be a moment in time when it is officially too late to do anything about how and to whom you leave the things you own. Even if you don't think you have a large estate, depending on the state you live in and how your assets are owned or structured, there are plenty of good reasons to think through your own estate plan.

At the very least, your last will and testament will spell out your final wishes, but each spouse has to have their own, since joint wills are not allowed. Nowadays, attorneys also include advance healthcare directives and a power of attorney document, in case you are incapacitated and can't communicate. You might spell out your "do not resuscitate" orders in your health care proxy, giving your spouse or other trusted person permission to pull the plug.

In addition, the power of attorney will grant powers to the person or persons you select to transact business on your behalf and make all kinds of other decisions should you not be able to do so yourself. None of this sounds fun, but by being proactive, you will be putting those you care about most and must ultimately leave behind in this world in a much better position than they would be with no plan at all.

The will also spells out what we call "who gets it and when" with regard to your property and other assets. The same goes for your beneficiary designations on retirement accounts and insurance policies. Are you sure these are up to date and reflect your current wishes?

With minor children or beneficiaries, a trust can come into play to protect them from other people taking advantage of them if you're not around, but it also protects them from themselves. If a minor inherits a large sum at a young age, it may impact their behavior and mindset in a way that you wouldn't approve of. Trusts can be set up to spread out any inheritances over different ages of maturity. It's common to see parents leave their children portions of the estate a third at a time at ages twenty-five, thirty, and thirty-five.

You know how in the airline safety spiel they always tell you to put the oxygen mask on yourself before you help others? Obviously, you can't help anyone if you go down first. All of the previous categories in this chapter have been about putting the oxygen mask on yourself. Once you've done that, you're able to focus on how you're going to help others, both while you're alive and after you're gone.

Besides making provisions for your family when you're gone, are there any charitable causes that are meaningful to you that you might want to contribute to, either as a legacy or while you are still living? If you have a large enough estate, you might trigger federal estate taxes upon your death, but there are a number of advanced planning strategies that you can employ to reduce, or even eliminate, your estate taxes while still being generous to your family and causes you care deeply about.

Your personal circumstances will dictate the level of estate planning complexity that you need to consider, but we believe nearly everyone in the runway decade should talk to an estate planning attorney and start tidying up their affairs to make sure their final wishes are spoken should the sun not come up tomorrow.

As a general rule, we believe you should review your estate plan every three to five years or whenever there is a major change in your life or family circumstances. If you haven't pulled your will out since your adult kids were in elementary school, now would be the time to do it.

ASSISTANCE TO OTHERS

Are there loved ones you will need to provide for throughout your retirement? This might include a parent or parents, especially if they are unable to provide for their own well-being. Do you have a child or other family member with special needs who will continue to need support even after your retirement? Do you have a plan in place for their care once you're gone?

We talked about this briefly when discussing the obstacles to overcome. It's not necessarily just about *needing* to provide financially for someone else, but it may be support that you are *wanting* to provide, such as funding the education needs of your kids or grandkids. Knowing how this impacts your plans and making some of these decisions now can keep you from leaving it to chance or someone else from having to decide for you when you're gone.

While unhealthy people can use money as a weapon, we prefer to see money as a form of love to be used to provide care for the people and causes most dear to your heart.

THE INTERCONNECTEDNESS OF YOUR MONEY

We've shared these seven categories of money as a way to help you wrap your head around every aspect of your financial planning, but we don't mean to suggest that this is a complete list or that these categories operate independently from each other. On the contrary, they are all deeply interconnected. The lines on the Financial Matrix don't just go up and down, they go sideways and diagonally across as well. Some of these connections are obvious; others are not. For example, cash flow and budgeting directly impact the amount of money you're saving and investing, and taxes, investing, and retirement all share common components.

Rather than thinking of these categories as separate buckets, it's better to think of money as an electrical current and the categories as circuits that the current passes through. Adjusting one category will impact others. They're all twisted and tied up together, so as you make decisions about each category, consider carefully how those decisions will make a broader impact on others. As we often say, "Money runs through just about everything."

For example, if you decide to change your investment profile, think about how it's going to affect things like income taxes, cash flow, retirement planning, and so on. If this gets confusing or too complex, consider seeking out the help of a professional who understands the interconnectedness and can simplify it and provide you with a big picture. That big picture can help you identify the areas that need more attention, as well as the trade-offs that have to be made along the way. The matrix we've provided will prove a useful tool as well. Just remember, anything in your life that touches a dollar needs to be addressed.

It would be nice if there was an easy way to get your matrix to automatically light up with colored lights: green to identify which categories are in good shape, yellow to identify which ones need a bit of attention, and red to identify which need immediate focus. If only there was a USB cord to plug into your brain and attach to the matrix, wouldn't it make things a lot easier? Since AI can't do this for you yet, it's up to you and your team of financial professionals to have the discussions and acquire the data you need to identify the areas that require the most focus.

At the very least, you need to have a heightened awareness about what's happening with your money in each of these seven categories, both now and in the future. Constantly ask yourself some version of "Do you know?" Get clarity and make intentional decisions during your runway decade so you can fill in the gaps and be in the best position possible as you head into retirement. To do that, you have to figure out what's working and what isn't working with your current financial plan in all of these crucial areas.

WHAT'S WORKING AND WHAT'S NOT WORKING?

"It isn't what we don't know that gives us
trouble, it's what we know that ain't so."

—Will Rogers

While reviewing a new potential client's tax returns, we discovered that the CPA who had done his taxes had made a major mistake with the client's stock option tax reporting. The mistake had cost him about $23,000 in additional taxes. Even though we're not CPAs, and we don't profess to be experts on stock options, we knew enough about how certain options are taxed that we were able to identify the problem and point it out to him so he could correct it.

We broke the news to the client gently, not knowing the depth of his relationship with his CPA. Rather than saying, "Hey, your CPA really messed this up," we took a more delicate, tactful approach. "You might want to ask your CPA to take another look at this. We're sure this was an honest mistake or an oversight, but knowing the type of options you have and how they are taxed, it looks like you were double-taxed on some of them. Your company taxed them as income when they granted you the options, and then your CPA added the full amount again to your income when you sold them, rather than just taxing the gain."

The client was justifiably shocked. "I just paid what I thought I owed," he said. "I never even questioned it." Of course, that's perfectly understandable. For one thing, many among us don't know enough to question the experts, and we're all terrified of the IRS anyway. Nobody wants to underpay their taxes or go through an audit, so sometimes people end up overpaying, don't realize they did it, and don't think twice about it.

Fortunately, there's generally a three-year window in which you can file an amended tax return, so he was able to re-file and get back all of the money he'd overpaid. But what if he'd gotten ten years down the road before discovering the mistake? Can you imagine the frustration of discovering that you paid the IRS $23,000 that you didn't owe, and now you can't do anything to get it back? That's $23,000 that could have been invested, earning a compounded return year after year—potential income that can never be recovered.

Now, you may not have complex stock options, but we've found other more common mistakes as well, and they can add up, even if just a few hundred or few thousand dollars. It's one reason why you want to gain clarity about what is working and what isn't working with your finances.

CLOSING THE GAPS

At this point, you've defined where you want to go, you've determined where you are now in your financial life, and you're trying to adopt healthier habits. Now, it's time to close the gaps in your financial plans so you can make progress toward your destination.

To do that, you're going to use your Financial Matrix from the previous chapter to conduct an audit of each category. We realize nobody likes to hear the word *audit*. Call it an x-ray or an MRI if you prefer, but the point is to get down to the real facts and actual truth about each topic.

It sounds about as fun as getting your teeth drilled, but unlike an IRS audit, this exercise isn't meant to hurt you or squeeze more money out of you.

On the contrary, the purpose of this exercise is to find any landmines in your current financial life so you can fix them before you accidentally or unknowingly step on them. You can conduct this audit yourself, or you can get professional help, but make sure you get through this exercise with a high degree of confidence about which categories need the most immediate attention.

If we use the colors green, yellow, and red to identify categories that are just fine (green), categories that need some attention (yellow), and categories that demand immediate focus (red), then your goal in this chapter is to turn each category from red or yellow to green. To do that, you might have to change some behaviors, buy some financial products or services, or seek out professional help.

As you go through each category, try to identify the financial and behavioral practices that need to improve or change. Let's tackle these one by one and pose some questions for you to think about and apply to your own situation.

Cash Flow and Budgeting

- Do you have an emergency fund set aside in cash reserves equal to at least three to six months' worth of your household expenses? Whatever the gap between your current reserves and your "margin of safety" number, make a plan to start nibbling away at it now.

- Are you holding this reserve money in a local bank, credit union, or brokerage money market account that is paying minuscule interest on your money compared to higher-yielding, FDIC-covered online bank options?

- Do you have memberships or subscriptions that you no longer use that can be canceled or refunded? What about other potential expenses mindlessly leaking out that you no longer care about? Apply these dollars to your other goals.

- Are you sure your mortgage, lines of credit, or other debts are taking advantage of the lowest interest rates? When was the last time you checked the market? Crunch the numbers to see if refinancing makes sense. Do you have an established plan for paying down your debts early? Monitor your debt-to-equity ratio and try to pay as little interest as possible over time while watching your cash flow.

- Besides saving for retirement income, are there other large purchases or expenses you anticipate that you need to set aside dollars for each month, like home improvements, a new car, or a vacation home? How much will you need and when? Set up and label a separate account for each goal and establish an automatic deposit so it is on cruise control.

- What is your personal savings rate? Do you need to start saving more of your salary? Determining your level of discretionary dollars you have each month after all expenses are accounted for helps guide how much you can safely save, spend, or give.

Maybe you'll discover that in order to reach your various goals, you have to change your personal savings rate. As discussed earlier, this has a huge impact on your investing success. A larger salary doesn't automatically translate to more money for retirement if your personal savings rate is too low.

Let's use a hypothetical situation. Suppose Claire makes $30,000 a year and saves 10 percent of her salary—that's $3,000 a year. Her neighbor Anne makes $100,000 a year but puts away 1 percent in her savings account—that's only $1,000. Even though Anne makes a much bigger salary, she is saving a lot less money each year, and that will translate to a lot less money for retirement.

Claire may not have a lot of room to cut her expenses any further, but with the higher income, it's more likely that Anne could. Furthermore, perhaps Anne's employer matches the first 3 percent of her salary that she defers into her company retirement plan, but she isn't even participating. If she just frees up cash flow to increase her deferral rate to 3 percent, her employer will kick in another 3 percent, giving her 6 percent of her salary overall going into her account each year.

Taking full advantage of your employer's "free money" is a great way to accelerate your savings. Are you leaving any of that on the table?

Investment Planning

As you get down to the "Do you know?" questions with regard to your investment planning and portfolio management, consider some of these items to measure your gaps:

- Do you have an updated investment policy statement that spells out your goals for the portfolio, the types of investments that you are okay using, and the targeted rate of risk and return you are comfortable with?

- Have you measured how your portfolio has performed versus its relative blended benchmark indexes? Knowing this can help you determine if you are at least experiencing an appropriate amount of return for the risk you're taking.

- Are your portfolio management fees in alignment with the marketplace for similarly sized portfolios? Paying for advice costs more than doing it yourself, but it's wise to know if you're getting what you're paying for. With a wide variety of fee structures across all different kinds of investments, this can be difficult to determine without some help, but it can also stop an unnecessary leak.

- Have you rebalanced your portfolio recently, or has your allocation gotten out of balance from a risk/return perspective due to market fluctuations? Staying in control of how your money is invested is among the greatest reasons to monitor your allocation periodically.

- Do you own funds that are substantially underperforming their peers in their asset class? It's not enough to diversify among asset classes.

You also need to make sure you have the best players available in each one.

The bigger your portfolio, the more opportunity there is for money to leak out, and the longer you go without knowing and closing the gaps, the harder your money has to work to compound like it should. Make some time to find out how these questions apply to your situation, and you'll be armed with the information to either check the box or change the course.

Retirement Planning

While there are many other areas that affect this one, the main purpose of this book is to inspire and motivate you to set yourself up for a great retirement. Here are some of the ways you can determine if you have gaps to close in this area:

- Do you have a fairly specific number in mind for how much you need to accumulate in retirement assets in order to comfortably retire and stay comfortably retired for thirty years or more?

- Have you conservatively projected your current account balances and current savings rate out to retirement to see how much you might have at different ages? How much will Social Security and pensions cover, and what is the annual income gap that needs to be filled?

- Are you fully taking advantage of your employer matching contributions?

- Are you able to defer more of your salary into your plan now that your kids are grown and some of your expenses have declined? This will not only accelerate your savings but also help lower your tax bill each year.

- If you are self-employed, have you explored all of your options for deferring income into your own retirement plan, whether a SEP, SIMPLE IRA, Solo 401(k), or cash balance pension plan?

- If you own a business with employees, do you know if you are leaving any money on the table by not having the most efficient plan design, like a cross-tested profit sharing plan paired with a safe harbor 401(k)?

- If you own your own business, or are a partner in a business, do you have an idea of your business exit strategy and how much your business is worth? What role will it play in your finances, and have you diversified properly by building assets outside of your business?

It is imperative that you determine how much income your money will reliably produce for you once the paychecks stop coming in, because this is going to determine the kind of lifestyle you can live throughout your retirement. How much income will you need to live your desired retirement lifestyle? How much of that income will be covered by Social Security and a pension? The income gap that remains will have to be covered by your savings.

As a simple shorthand example, let's say your annual expenses in retirement come to $100,000, and between Social Security and your annual pension, $55,000 of it is covered. Assuming you aren't earning any other income, your portfolio will have to provide the other $45,000. If we assume a withdrawal rate of 4.5 percent on your money, then $45,000 divided by .045 equals $1,000,000. As a rough draft, that's the amount you'd need to accumulate to retire at your $100,000 per year lifestyle. Likewise, if you need a portfolio that produces all $100,000 with no help from other sources, you'd need around $2,220,000 saved by your retirement date.

Projecting your current values along with your additions at a conservative rate of return, let's say you're only estimated to have $900,000 of the $1,000,000 you need by your retirement date. You'll have to make up the difference by saving more each month, taking more risk to try and earn a better rate of return, or extending your retirement date out to give you more time to hit your number. Making the runway longer is not the worst thing that can happen if you're unable to increase your personal savings rate enough.

Income Tax Planning

We opened this chapter with a real-life story about a relatively large amount of tax money that was almost lost forever, only to be found in time and recovered. More common is the smaller "death by a thousand cuts" of mistakes and oversights. It's not a bad idea to get a second set of eyes on your last two or three years' worth of tax returns, so you can see if you have any gaps in this area:

- Are you taking all of the deductions and getting all of the credits you're eligible for each year? These put tax dollars directly back into your pocket.

- Are you wisely and proactively harvesting any current year or carry-forward losses against any of your unrealized gains? If you have large concentrated stock positions that you'd like to reduce or eliminate your allocation to, knowing your tax basis and the amount of your offsetting losses can help you make good decisions and save you tax money.

- Are you fully maximizing your deductible retirement plan contributions and health savings account contributions, if available? Are you balancing building your personal taxable investments with pre-tax, tax-deferred alternatives that will help lower your tax bill?

- If you are in one of the higher tax brackets, are you making use of tax-free municipal bonds for some of your fixed income allocation?

- If you own your own business, are you aware of all of the legitimate business write-offs you can take to avoid unnecessary taxes?

- If you are philanthropically minded and have the extra cash from a big income year, have you set up your own foundation or a donor-advised fund to get a charitable gift deduction?

Like the client in our opening story, make sure you aren't paying *more* than your fair share of taxes. We're all entitled to certain legal tax reduction strategies the government has established, so make sure you're capitalizing on them. Through a simple review of your tax returns, you might uncover potential deductions, credits, or other strategies to reduce your overall taxes, as long as you know where to look. Remember, the greater your income, the more impact a missed tax-reduction opportunity will make.

Risk Management and Insurance

The questions in this section could be many, but they come down to a few basics:

- Do you know what would happen financially to your family or your business if you or your spouse, partner, or key employee didn't wake up tomorrow? What commitments have been made that would need to be taken care of and have they been adequately funded or at least insured?

- The same goes for you or any of the above becoming disabled tomorrow and being unable to work going forward. How would the loss of income affect you, your family, or your business?

- Have you considered what would happen financially if you or your spouse required extended home health services or had to be admitted to a long-term care facility? If not self-funded, how would you expect to pay for the care, and how would that impact the longevity of your assets for the healthy spouse's long-term needs?

- Have you updated your coverage for any property you own and talked with your insurance agent about potential liability losses in the case of accidents that may welcome lawsuits?

There is a cost to procrastination. Every day you don't address a known issue, you get a little older and a little less insurable, the runway gets smaller, and the cost of insurance goes up. It goes without saying, but you buy auto insurance *before* you get in a wreck. You buy homeowner's insurance *before* your house burns down. You buy flood insurance *before* the river beside your property crests its banks. And you prepare for your long-term financial needs before you get close to retirement.

If you look at an airport runway from the sidelines, it seems very long, with plenty of room for even a massive jumbo jet to build up speed and take off. The average commercial airline runway is between 8,000 and 13,000 feet long. That's roughly 1.5 to 2.5 miles!

But when you're sitting in the cockpit staring at the runway in front of you, suddenly it doesn't seem nearly so long, and when you're barreling down the runway toward takeoff at 160 to 180 miles per hour, it all passes by pretty fast. Procrastinate even for a moment and a large segment of the runway will pass you by in a blur.

As the old soap opera used to say, "Like sands through the hourglass, so are the days of our lives." When the last grain of "regret" will drop is anyone's guess. Keep in mind as well that the cost of a solution is typically a lot less than the cost of the problem—most of the time, just a fraction.

We ran into a situation several years ago where two people each owned a 50 percent stake in a company worth around $10 million. Their operating agreement stipulated that if one of them died, the other was contractually obligated to buy out the rest of the company from the heirs over no more than five years.

So if one died, the other had to come up with $5 million to pay the deceased member's family over five years. They had an obligation to each other, but no funding mechanism other than taking it out of cash flow, personal assets, or a big loan. However, none of those provided as efficient a solution as purchasing a $5 million life insurance policy on each other.

That life insurance policy might have cost them $5,000 a year each, which sounds like a lot of money, but it paled in comparison to $5 million each. Indeed, they would have had to pay 1,000 years of premiums before they got to $5 million, but all they really needed to do was bridge the gap and cover the problem until they sold the company within the next ten years or so.

The same is true of long-term care and disability insurance. If you become disabled at fifty, you will miss out on fifteen years of work and earning a salary. If your salary is $100,000 a year, your problem is the sum total of $1.5 million of lost income by the time you reach retirement. Your cost? A small monthly premium that likely doesn't even add up to 1 percent of your annual salary.

When it comes to managing risk and buying insurance, the gap you need to cover is the cost of the problem. The premium you'll have to fork over is simply the much smaller cost of the solution.

Estate Planning and Charitable Giving

We'll spare you another hourglass analogy and get right to the questions to help you determine your gaps in this area:

- Do you have a valid will in the state you currently live in and have you reviewed it in the past three to five years, or since any major changes to your situation?

- Put simply, who do you want to get your stuff? When and how are they going to get it? As it stands right now, are you happy with the way everything would flow at your death?

- Have you had to help out one child so much more than another during your life that you wish to even things up at your death when your estate is settled? Do you have specific things you want to leave to specific people?

- Have you appointed someone to make legal, business, and healthcare decisions for you if you're unable to do so yourself?

- If you are the legal guardian for your children or grandchildren, have you hand-picked your successor to take over these duties when you're gone?

- Have you named a trustee or someone to manage your financial matters on behalf of your heirs, or do you want everyone to get the full share of your estate at your death?

- Do you have plans to leave a legacy to a favorite cause when you're gone?

- If you have substantial assets, have you taken steps to make sure that your estate won't be needlessly taxed away by the government at your death? Might your family have to sell something you don't want them to sell to come up with the money?

- Have you considered burial plots and plans ahead of time?

Through a properly drafted will, you have the ability to "speak from the grave" about your final wishes. You can protect your loved ones from other people, and even from themselves. At the very least, you can leave your family a plan instead of a disorganized mess to figure out.

We always tell clients you do this type of work because you love people. You don't do it for yourself, because clearly you won't be around to see any of it happen.

Assistance to Others

Along those same lines, the people you care about most not only need assistance after you're gone, they need it while you're alive and can derive enjoyment out of seeing the fruits of your labor and generosity. Here are a few thoughts to consider as we wrap up the audit of your matrix:

- Are you concerned your children aren't developing good money habits? Do you have adult children who still need your financial help from time to time, and if so, do you know how this is impacting your own retirement plan?

- Who do you need or want to help educate, and what will that cost? How much will you need and when?

- Are your parents or spouse's parents still living, and do you expect to have to provide for their care at some point? Do you have siblings who could share in the cost or care duties?

THE FINANCIAL CONFIDENCE QUADRANT

To help you audit your financial categories, we've created the following Financial Confidence Quadrant. You can easily make this on a notebook page, or you can go to *www. runwaydecade.com* and download a blank template. Use it to identify which things are working well right now in your financial plans, and which things need to be tweaked, adjusted, or changed completely.

THE FINANCIAL CONFIDENCE QUADRANT

	KNOWN	UNKNOWN

POSITIVES	Things you are doing well or on the right track with that you know about
	
	1. _____
	   _____
	
	2. _____
	   _____
	
	3. _____
	   _____
	
	4. _____
	   _____
	
	5. _____
	   _____
		Things you are doing well or on the right track with but you are unaware
		
		1. _____
		   _____
		
		2. _____
		   _____
		
		3. _____
		   _____
		
		4. _____
		   _____
		
		5. _____
		   _____

NEGATIVES	Things you need to address, resolve, fix, improve, or get rid of that you know about
	
	1. _____
	   _____
	
	2. _____
	   _____
	
	3. _____
	   _____
	
	4. _____
	   _____
	
	5. _____
	   _____
		Things you need to address, resolve, fix, improve, or get rid of but are unaware
		
		1. _____
		   _____
		
		2. _____
		   _____
		
		3. _____
		   _____
		
		4. _____
		   _____
		
		5. _____
		   _____

Let's define each quadrant.

- **Known Positives**—These are the things you are doing well or are on the right track with *that you know about* (e.g., you have no debt except a mortgage, *and* you're paying extra principal each month; you're enrolled in your employer's retirement plan *and* saving 10 percent or more of salary; your cash reserves are equal to at least three months of living expenses).

- **Known Negatives**—These are things you need to address, resolve, fix, improve, or get rid of *that you know about* (e.g., you are not adequately funding your kids' college accounts; the retirement account at your former employer is not being monitored or managed; you don't have an updated will that reflects your current wishes and wealth picture).

- **Unknown Positives**—These are things you are doing well or are on the right track with, but *you are unaware of them* (e.g., your income-to-expense ratio is in line; your retirement projections to age sixty-five suggest you can retire comfortably at that age; the money manager for your IRA is among the best in their class for risk-adjusted returns).

- **Unknown Negatives**—These are things you need to address, resolve, fix, improve, or get rid of, but *you are unaware of them* (e.g., your life insurance proceeds and non-retirement savings and investments aren't enough to sustain your family's lifestyle if you died today; your overall asset allocation is too overlapped and conservative to meet your desired rate of return requirements; you are leaving valuable tax deductions on the table each year).

Now that you have pondered the questions in each section of the matrix, use this as an opportunity to think through the specific areas of your financial life and plot them in what you feel is the correct quadrant. For example, if you know you need to update your will, put that under "Known Negatives." If you are 100 percent certain that your life insurance beneficiaries are up to date, put that one under "Known Positives," and so forth. The ultimate goal is to get all of these thoughts down, placing every area of your financial life in whatever quadrant it may fall so you can move it toward the "Known Positives" section.

The real challenge of this process will be those items in the unknown quadrants, especially the "Unknown Negatives." These are the problems that you're simply not aware of, so they can be difficult to identify on your own. However, as the old saying goes, "Ignorance is not a defense." Pete still recalls, some thirty-five years later, his LSU business law professor explaining in his slow southern drawl, "Ignorance defined as 'not knowing' is not a defense because you *knew* that you didn't *know*." At least if you know that you don't know, you can seek out the information, make the adjustment, or ask for help.

Even someone who is knowledgeable and highly disciplined can have blind spots when it comes to financial matters. As the saying goes, "You can't read the label from inside the jar." Sometimes, you need an outside set of eyes to see your assumptions, emotional decisions, and blind spots. None of us can fully appreciate all the perspectives we need for the simple fact that we live inside of our own viewpoint every single day.

Even if your financial plan is 90 percent perfect and optimized, a good coach or advisor can add crucial perspective on that final 10 percent. The greatest athletes in the world have coaches for this very reason. Did Tiger Woods really need a swing coach at the peak of his career? Absolutely, because he needed someone with expertise to do the one thing he could not do himself: hold up a mirror and show him things about his performance that he couldn't see on his own.

At the same time, even if you know that something is working well, you have to avoid becoming complacent about it or putting it on autopilot. A category can shift from green to yellow to red while you're not paying attention, moving from a "Known Positive" to an "Unknown Negative." This isn't just about crunching numbers. Certainly, there's the well-known mathematical component to closing the gaps in your financial confidence, but there are also the non math components. Sometimes the "Known Negatives" are emotions—like fear, whether real or imagined—or they can be the ugly counterpart of FOMO (fear of missing out). As you do this exercise, whether by yourself or with someone, you'll have to address the emotional side of your financial behavior in order to make the best decisions.

Then again, don't forget that any actual math you do to figure out how much you're going to accumulate by retirement is based, in part, on assumption. As Yogi Berra said, "It's tough to make predictions, especially about the future." We can't know with absolute certainty what the future holds. The only reliable guide we have is historical performance. We can examine how things have performed in the past, make some assumptions about the likely performance in the future, then adjust along the way if things don't go as we expected.

Remember, something is working if it's bringing you closer to your financial and retirement goals. Anything that isn't moving you toward your goals needs to be corrected now, while you still have runway left. Whether it's overpaying taxes, risk mitigation, or better saving and investing, there is power in knowing what's working and not working in your financial life.

Now that you have some idea of what needs to be changed, improved, added, or deleted, you can begin finding specific ways to build wealth in order to reach your destination with confidence. Next, we'll look at some of the vehicles you can use to help you get there.

WAYS TO GET THERE

"Among the four most dangerous words in
investing are 'it's different this time.'"
—Sir John Templeton

n the introduction, we established the current life expec-
tancies of men and women born around 1967 (age eighty
and eighty-three respectively) and explained that it is reasonable for you to plan to beat those odds. As you ponder
the various vehicles and strategies for accumulating the
resources you'll need to produce monthly income when
the paychecks stop, it is important to consider how long
you may live after you retire.

Put another way, the threshold question is, "How long will I need my money to last?"

If you're fifty years old, it's understandable to look at life expectancy and say, "Oh, men live to be eighty, and women live to be eighty-three, so I should plan for that many years, maybe with a little margin for error so we don't run out."

First, it's not an exact science, and who really knows when you'll see your last sunrise? Second, the reality is, you should be planning for much longer, and the stats actually back that up. The average joint life expectancy of a sixty-two-year-old couple today (the age when the last death would occur) is ninety-two.[9] Again, as we continue to reiterate, this is just the average, which means that even setting aside leaving a legacy, we recommend having a plan in place that can support you and your spouse for *thirty years plus* after retirement.

The idea is to have you think differently about your time horizon in your fifties, not just to retirement but through it. Many people do the math between their current age and their retirement age and start to invest too conservatively too soon when they may have thirty to forty years or more left to live.

---

9   IRS Updated Life Expectancy and Distribution Period Tables Used for Purposes of Determining Minimum Required Distributions, *Joint and Last Survivor Table*, 11/12/2020

So, if we accept that premise at face value, then the next obvious question is, "How do I make sure there will be enough resources to last that long?"

The first part of that answer, which we touched on previously, is to have a plan. Just like planning for any kind of endeavor, it helps to know what you're up against.

In planning for a thirty-year retirement, perhaps your biggest enemy is inflation. For as long as you have been alive, even going back into the 1930s and 1940s when many of our parents were born, the cost of goods and services, as measured by the consumer price index (CPI), has compounded at a rate of around three percent per year. That means that over the course of a thirty-year retirement, the cost of living will increase by close to two and a half times. If you were born in 1970, a gallon of milk cost your parents $1.32 on average. Today, you're paying almost $4. That, in a nutshell, is inflation.

Of course, it's natural to think, "If I have to plan for thirty years of retirement, then I'd better play it safe!" But the reality is, you can go broke "safely," as we like to say. If you just park a bunch of money in a non-interest-generating account, or a coffee can, thinking that will keep it safe, your money will slowly lose its value over time due to inflation. All you would have done is protected the units of currency that you have—the actual paper and coins—but you would not have protected the value of what those units of currency could buy.

A hundred-dollar bill still looks like a hundred-dollar bill after it's been sitting in a drawer for thirty years, but when you take it to the grocery store, and your $4 box of Frosted Flakes today costs around $10 then, you'll realize a little too late that your hundred-dollar bill was withering away quietly all those years down to about forty dollars. In the end, money is only what it can buy, so how "safe" was the drawer or mayonnaise jar after all, when the only logical conclusion you can draw from this is that it lost you the equivalent of sixty dollars?

Not to pile on, but right now somewhere in America, there's a ninety-year-old who retired thirty years ago and stuffed a bunch of money in her mattress, thinking she was keeping it safe. She never invested it, so it never earned any interest, dividends, or growth. If she'd pulled a dollar out of that jar in 1992 and went down to the local post office to buy stamps, that single dollar would have been enough to buy three stamps with a few pennies left over.

Today, at ninety, if she pulls a dollar out of the jar and heads to the post office, she's only going to be able to afford one stamp with change. The same dollar bill that used to buy three now only buys one! Effectively, this woman has lost money. No, she didn't lose the actual paper currency, but its value has dropped dramatically over time. We say again, that's all money is: what it can buy.

Since 1965, inflation has produced a cumulative price increase of 782.37 percent, which makes today's prices 8.82 times higher than prices in 1965.[10] Looking at it another way, a dollar today only buys 11.33 percent of what it could buy back then. You wouldn't be too far off to say, "a dollar ain't worth a dime anymore!" So, all of that money under the mattress has lost a tremendous amount of purchasing power, and it's only going to continue leaking value as long as it stays there.

Inflation is an insidious, invisible force that slowly but relentlessly erodes the purchasing power of your money. So you don't need to invest simply to gain more money, you need to invest to compensate for the erosive power of inflation on your dollars. If you don't use some investment vehicle to accumulate wealth up to and throughout your retirement, you will lose money even without spending a dime.

Inflation is indeed enemy number one. When it comes to slaying this dragon, nothing has historically compared

---

10   Ian Webster, "The U.S. dollar has lost 89% of its value since 1965," Official Data Foundation, updated February 10, 2022, https://www.in2013dollars.com/us/inflation/1965.

to owning shares of the great companies of America and the world. But, more on that just ahead. First, we need to make sure we are all using the same definitions to describe the features of our various investment options.

RISK VS. VOLATILITY

Enemy number two is usually a person's mindset around terms like "risk" and "volatility" because it impacts their investment choices. When asked, most people define risk as "the chance of losing all my money." We would agree, but by "money" they mean their principal, and we mean their purchasing power. Now that you've seen that even money sitting safely in a coffee can or savings account with no risk to the principal is capable of losing its value over time, you can start to think about risk differently.

When a pilot is headed for a specific destination, there are usually a number of different flight paths they can take to get there. Some will be better and safer than others because of varying weather, wind, and air traffic. Similarly, when you have a long-term financial destination in mind, there are multiple ways to reach it. Some will be quicker but perhaps with more bumps along the way. Others will be slower but smoother sailing and may leave you wondering if you will ever get there at all.

THE MYTH OF THE COFFEE CAN

We talk a lot about the impact of inflation on the value of currency, but rarely do we get to see a real-life long-term "coffee can" field study on public display. In 2006, a Cleveland-area contractor named Bob Kitts was doing some renovation work for homeowner Amanda Reece in an eighty-three-year-old home when he found a couple of metal boxes containing $182,000 in 1920s US currency hidden behind a wall, hanging by a wire from the medicine cabinet. Initially elated, Bob and Amanda decided to split the money, but they disagreed on the amount. Ultimately, a very public fight ensued and the case wound up in court, drawing the attention of the twenty-one heirs of the home's previous owner, a wealthy Depression-era businessman named Patrick Dunne. Being perfectly human, every heir wanted a share of the wealth.

Unfortunately, by the time the heirs crawled out of the woodwork, most of the money was long gone, spent on lavish Hawaiian vacations and other luxuries. The amount that was finally dispersed by the court was fairly small, then quickly spent by the heirs. It's actually kind of a sad case of lost opportunity. Like so many lottery winners, Amanda and Bob actually wound up worse off in the end than if they'd never come across the money, thanks to court costs. Amanda Reece apparently eventually filed for bankruptcy.

continued...

...continued

Imagine if Patrick Dunne hadn't put that money in the wall to begin with. We can all sympathize with him for making this decision during the Great Depression, when banks were collapsing all around him, and joblessness was headed for all-time highs. The stock market had experienced a historic crash in 1929, and it seemed like Armageddon was just around the corner. Perhaps hiding money behind a wall in his home was a panic-driven decision meant to protect himself and his family from an unprecedented catastrophe. Ironically though, Patrick Dunne never actually needed that money, which is why it stayed hanging in that wall until 2006, some 40 years after his death in 1966.

If we take inflation into account, that $182,000 was the equivalent of around $2.1 million back in 1929. In order to have maintained its purchasing power until 2006 when it was discovered, that's how much it would have had to grow. Except it didn't—and couldn't—grow because it sat behind a wall, quietly eroding in value over time due to the insidious, invisible tax called inflation.

To quote Yogi Berra again, "A nickel ain't worth a dime anymore." Technically, for Patrick Dunne's money, a dollar was worth about 9 cents by the time it was found compared to when it went in. Good thing it was "safe" from the banks and the

continued...

market while it was tucked away with no "risk." That's a huge loss in value, and that's just comparing it to what it needed to be worth today to break even.

Now, let's suppose that instead of hiding it behind a wall, Dunne had put that money in a trust that similarly couldn't be touched for eighty-three years and then invested it. He would have been investing at the mother of all buying opportunities, when the Dow Jones was down to around 100. Even if he'd only netted an 8 percent compounded return after taxes, that trust would have been worth more than $108 million in 2006, and the heirs wouldn't have had to come crawling out of the woodwork to get a piece of it. The trust would already have been assigned to them, setting up a huge multigenerational legacy.

Yes, it was still a lot of money to find even in modern times, but not only did it lose almost all of its original value, it ultimately lost 100 percent of its potential to support, help, or do good for others.

Somehow, you have to design an investment strategy that will build enough wealth and security to compensate for inflation and provide a growing income that will last throughout your retirement years. It's not an easy choice, and there are a dizzying array of options. There are so many financial products and investment opportunities: fixed, indexed, and variable annuities, cash value life insurance, stocks, bonds, mutual funds, exchange-traded funds (ETFs), cash, alternative investments, real estate, and much more. It can be confusing to decide which ones are right for you, much less how to blend them together in the optimal way for what you are trying to accomplish.

These opportunities exist across a broad spectrum of risk and return, so you also have to match the right vehicle with each specific goal and then decide how comfortable (or uncomfortable) you are with enduring their price swings. More on that in a minute. Just remember, you're trying to protect and grow your purchasing power, not just the principal you invest.

What usually causes people to avoid investing is a fear of losing all of their money in a bad investment, but let's be clear: even though they are often mentioned together, *volatility* and *risk* are two very different things. Yes, we've seen some huge companies go belly up over the years, and people lost all they invested in those companies. Any individual company can crash and burn, and take their investors' money down with them. If, for some ill-advised reason, you invest most or all of your money into the stock of a single company, that's the chance you'd take. That's *risky*.

However, no sound investment approach involves putting all of your eggs into one basket, or all of your money into a single company. Managed investment portfolios, mutual funds, and ETFs are diversified across dozens, even hundreds, of companies, providing safety against one bad apple spoiling the bunch. Think of it this way: if you had a bundle of twenty pencils bound together with a rubber band and pulled out a single pencil, you could snap it in your hands without any trouble. That's one company. However, if you grab the whole bundle of pencils and try to snap all of them at once, it's practically impossible. That's a diversified portfolio of companies.

While any single company could possibly collapse for all kinds of reasons, it is extremely unlikely that a whole bunch of diversified companies across a variety of different industries will do so at the same time. In fact, the Standard & Poor's (S&P) 500 Index gives us a great glimpse into that exact possibility over many years, crises, political chapters, and world events.

The S&P 500 Index is an unmanaged index representing 500 of the world's most successful, best-managed, and well-financed publicly traded companies. That's not twenty pencils in a bundle, it's 500! It started in 1923 as a composite index of ninety companies and was updated to its current number of 500 companies in 1957. So, whether we look back to the founding of the original index nearly a hundred years ago, or merely use the current version from sixty-five years ago, there are enough different versions of the "end of the world" in the years between then and now to give us a solid sample size of possible results and potential catastrophic failures.

And with all the wars, disasters, epidemics, assassinations, and more in America and the world over that time frame, how many times do you think all the pencils snapped and went bankrupt at the same time?

Hint: It's a nice round number.

If you said, "Zero," you would be exactly right. It may be *possible*, but it would take an absolutely unprecedented event of apocalyptic proportions for all 500 of those companies to crash and burn simultaneously. It's never happened. It's never come close to happening. *Possible* perhaps, but not remotely *probable*, with history as our guide. Plus, if every stock of every company goes to zero on the same day, and all of them go out of business at the same time, you're not going to be worried about your money—you're going to be worried about how many bullets you have in your gun to survive the apocalypse!

Seriously though, all that is to say, if the fear of invest-ing in stocks is based on "losing all my money in the stock market," then—at least so far—in a properly diversified portfolio, that fear, that risk, is imagined and not real. It's a myth. It's never happened.

On the other hand, *volatility* happens all the time in the financial markets as a whole every year. It is to be expected, anticipated, even encouraged, but it tends to have a neg-ative connotation, and many people see it as a synonym for "loss" or "downturn." The truth is that the volatility of a stock (or index of stocks) simply refers to the variability of prices around their trend line, both up and down. In general, if an investment can't go down very much, it likely won't be able to go up very much either.

The average intra-year decline for the S&P 500 Index going back to 1980 was -13.5 percent, representing the aver-age maximum price declines per year. All the while, the index averaged over 12 percent gains per year with dividends reinvested. Some years, at their lowest point, were down as much as 34 percent, and during the depths of the 2008 credit crisis and recession, it bottomed out down 49 percent.[11]

11   FactSet, Standard & Poors, JP Morgan Asset Management "Guide to the Markets," as of February 28, 2022, https://am.jpmorgan. com/us/en/asset-management/adv/insights/market-insights/ guide-to-the-markets.

While it has, thus far, only been temporary, that is volatility in a nutshell. A diversified stock portfolio can and will *go* down, but it's never *stayed* down. Being able to accept and expect it as part of the tradeoff to achieving the greater long-term potential returns of stocks is vital to being an equity investor. Nor can you really try to time it or outguess which way it will turn. According to a study by J.P. Morgan, six of the ten best-performing days for the stock market occurred within two weeks of the ten worst days.[12]

Volatility is the friend of the patient long-term accumulator of capital. In fact, volatility is the very reason that stocks go up over time, because historically they have gone up much more than they have gone down. As Morgan Housel puts it, "Volatility is not a fine, it's a fee you pay for long-term returns."

According to J.P. Morgan's most recent *Guide to the Markets*, from 1926 through 2021, the S&P 500 Index, with dividends reinvested, has posted a positive return in:

- 75.72 percent of rolling one-year periods
- 88.29 percent of rolling five-year periods

---

12   Michael Aloi, "What Happens When You Miss the Best Days in the Stock Market," The Motley Fool, April 11, 2019, https://www. fool.com/investing/2019/04/11/what-happens-when-you-miss-the-best-days-in-the-st.aspx.

ANNUAL RETURNS AND PULLBACKS

S&P 500 Index

This chart shows the performance of the stock market (bars) and the largest intra-year decline (dots) each year.

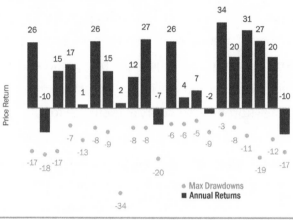

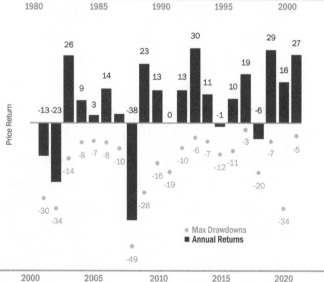

- 94.48 percent of rolling ten-year periods
- 99.69 percent of rolling fifteen-year periods
- 100 percent of rolling twenty-year periods[13]

Once you get to seventeen-year rolling periods and longer, there hasn't been a single period of negative returns. Put another way, the risk of losing principal in a broadly diversified portfolio of stocks has fallen to zero over time.

Enduring short-term volatility in exchange for the opportunity for greater long-term gains is the price of investing, but it's usually more of an emotional price than a financial one. Being able to stomach seeing your statements or account balance online with a lower number than when you last looked is part of the price of admission.

From February 19 to March 23, 2020, the market dropped precipitously in response to COVID-19 lockdowns. The entire global economy and supply chains were disrupted in ways that they had never been before. Some people panicked and dumped all of their investments, convinced that the sky was falling. However, with unprecedented levels of human ingenuity, cooperation, and innovation, the market soon recovered and continued its advance.

---

13   JP Morgan Asset Management "Guide to the Markets."

Many who had sold their shares were unable to get back in at the same price, so they lost money *and* missed out on growth—all because they gave in to the panic and made an assumption that somehow this time would be different than the past big pullbacks and not ever come back. Legendary investor Sir John Templeton said, "Among the four most dangerous words in investing are 'it's different this time.'" The circumstances are always different, and the big pullbacks always feel terrible to endure, but innovative and enduring companies ultimately adapt, adjust, and recover, and their share prices tend to eventually follow.

It's important to point out that "the market" did not create losses for the people who sold in fear. The investors did that all by themselves. Stocks eventually recovered and soared to new heights, and all an investor had to do to experience all of that return was to sit still and do nothing. The key to doing nothing is to expect volatility, not get surprised by it, and therefore not react to it. Remember what veteran advisor and author Nick Murray said: "Surprise is the mother of all panic." Panicking turns temporary declines into permanent losses, and that is a purely human thing, not a market thing.

So far, we have redefined "risk" and "loss" from a *protection of principal* definition to a *protection of purchasing power* definition. Investments are risky if they erode our purchasing power. We have also unlinked volatility from risk and loss, and we understand now that it is as normal as the birds chirping in the spring. With those arrows in our quiver, we can now talk more about the different vehicles people use to save for retirement and discuss ways to tell which ones might be best for you in your own unique situation.

PICKING THE BEST TOOL FOR THE JOB

Along the journey between now and your final sunrise—hopefully decades from now—you will continue to require a variety of different accounts to best manage your financial life and meet your goals. Those accounts will vary in terms of their purpose and the timing of when you need access to them, so it's important to match the right tool with the right job. Often, we encounter situations where people are effectively bringing a knife to a gunfight, so to speak.

Beyond the checking account that you use to receive deposits and pay your bills, we believe you should maintain a year's worth of living expenses in a savings account or money market fund. Set this aside for emergencies, also for temporary unemployment and job changes, or even to bridge the income gap until your disability benefits kick in if you can't work.

Search for the highest-yielding account with FDIC coverage, which these days is typically offered online by some of the big reputable financial companies. Don't assume that whoever you have your checking account with offers the best rate. We addressed this earlier as "money leaking out." It happens when a large balance is needlessly parked in checking or local bank savings accounts effectively making zero interest, even as hundreds or thousands of dollars of interest is there for the taking with a couple of clicks on the web or via an app. No, you don't have time to overcome any swings to your principal and shouldn't invest these dollars, but you should safely earn the highest interest that you can.

Bonds

If you have a shorter-term goal that requires withdrawing a lump sum of money within the next five years or so, you should consider investing that money in *bonds* or notes that correspond with when you anticipate needing it. Typically, you can earn higher interest rates than money market accounts without much volatility or risk to your principal. Bonds can also fluctuate in value, but the shorter maturity or duration the bonds are, the less the prices tend to swing. Plus, a negative year in bonds is rare and, even then, a negative year in bonds is more like a negative week in stocks.

Bonds are debt instruments issued by federal and state governments, municipalities, or corporations when they want to borrow money. When you buy a bond, you are in essence giving the issuer a loan, and they agree to pay you back the value of the loan after a defined period of time, along with periodic "rent" payments along the way. For example, if you invest $10,000 for a five-year bond or note, the issuer might pay 1 or 2 percent a year ($100 to $200) for those five years, and then, at the end of the five years, you get your $10,000 back. Now, due to inflation, that $10,000 is going to buy a little less after five years than when you invested in the bond in the first place, but over such short periods of time, the effect on purchasing power is much less and is a fair tradeoff since you require your principal so soon.

Again, we are talking about lump sums needed within five years or so, not income. Some examples might be the down payment on a vacation property or college tuition due within a few years.

For all of us on the pre-retirement runway with multiple years to go, we believe that any amount of capital that does not fall into either the liquid emergency bucket, or the "I need it within five years" bucket, should be invested in a diversified portfolio of company stocks, which we often refer to as equities.

Once you are on or across the doorstep of retirement, we would suggest bumping the money market balance from one year's worth of living expenses to one-and-a-half to two years' worth. The purpose of this increase is to give yourself a bigger cushion to avoid having to draw from your equity portfolio during inevitable periods of market decline. That way, you can avoid selling shares at a bad time and give them time to recover. After all, you will be in distribution mode rather than accumulation mode, without paychecks coming in, so you'll need a higher margin of safety.

Before we get to the compelling answer for "why stocks?" as the best long-term wealth accumulation vehicle, let's spend a minute or two discussing some of the other tools we've seen misused for that job.

Cash-Value Life Insurance

First and foremost, there's *cash-value life insurance*, often referred to as whole life or universal life. While this certainly has a place in the financial planning tool kit to guard against the chance of dying too soon, it's not the best tool for long-term wealth-building. Whole life is typically sold as a conservative and tax-advantaged way to save money to live on in retirement because the interest or dividends that the insurance companies pay grow tax-deferred until withdrawn, and the cash value can be withdrawn via tax-free policy loans. Both of these things are true.

The problems we have run into are two-fold. First, because of mortality charges and policy expenses, the money typically only compounds at a low single-digit return, maybe around 2 to 3 percent annually. Variable universal life insurance uses investment managers to offer stock and bond subaccounts as the accumulation vehicle inside the policy, but the returns are still impacted by the policy fees. Second, in over thirty years of practice, we've never encountered anyone living on their life insurance cash value. Not one. Those people are surely out there somewhere, and perhaps the strategy worked for their situation, but we've never encountered it.

Granted, we've seen huge and timely needs for policy death benefits when someone passed away, and the legitimate cases for permanent insurance coverage versus term insurance are many. However, not a single person out of thousands we've met has relied on cash-value life insurance as a meaningful income stream the way it is often sold to them—even those with large cash balances in them. In fact, most people end up liquidating the policies or using the accumulated cash for some other goal along the way.

We have our theories about this from years of advising clients, but for the most part, the people who can afford to overfund life insurance policies to build up cash are also able to accumulate plenty of value in retirement plans, stocks, real estate, and other assets. By the time they get to retirement, they often find that they don't even need the cash value—or at least, it is the last place they go for income. If they don't use it, it will likely come out as a death benefit, which could have been purchased for much smaller premiums over those many years.

If you already have substantial cash value built up in an insurance policy, we would encourage you to have the agent or company run what is called an "in-force illustration." What that report will typically show is that as you take out the payments, the death benefit will also start to drop in the later years. Many people have the expectation that they will take out all of the cash and still have the full death benefit for their heirs, but this is often not the case.

That's all well and good if you have gone in with eyes wide open, but we find that has seldom been the case. In fact, it's usually more a case of an insurance agent not having all the tools available in their tool chest. The situation calls for a hammer, but all they have is a screwdriver, so they turn it around and use the handle to start beating the nail. Or as the old saying goes, "If all you have is a hammer, everything looks like a nail!"

If you're just going around the corner to your buddy's house, taking your bike is okay. If you live in Boston and your buddy lives in Los Angeles, taking your bike is a terrible idea, and you may not even get there! Heck, depending on how fast and safely you need to get there, even taking your car may not be ideal. You'll need a plane for that one.

Deferred and Immediate Annuities

Similarly, we find people using short-term investment vehicles in accounts with long-term time horizons. For instance, countless times we've run into folks with their IRA account in a twelve-month certificate of deposit (CD) at their bank. They won't need it for twenty more years, but they have it invested as if they'll need it next year.

Likewise, we run across all sorts of fixed annuities, which may have paid a high first-year teaser rate, but now pay only 1 to 2 percent on money set aside for retirement way beyond the runway. Annuities are issued by insurance companies and come in all sorts of confusing types, shapes, and sizes, but their main utility is to serve as a guaranteed income source in an overall retirement income plan. While life insurance covers you if you die too soon, annuities are said to cover you if you live too long. It's a strange way to put it, but in essence, as long as the insurance company making the guarantee is solvent, annuity payments can be set up to last until you die, ensuring that you won't outlive your money.

Besides fixed annuities that simply credit you with an interest rate each year while accumulating, equity index annuities and variable annuities earn money differently. This is an overgeneralization because annuity contracts vary from company to company, but most equity index annuities protect your principal from earning less than zero in a given year in exchange for capping your upside potential based on a percentage of the market index it is linked to (for instance, the S&P 500 Index we discussed earlier). The money is not invested directly into the market, but the amount of earnings credited to your contract is based on the performance of the market. Because of this feature, they have historically earned more than simple fixed interest annuities.

There are simply too many flavors of these products to explore in detail here, but in an attempt to simplify, that's how they usually work.

Variable annuities typically have a multitude of investment choices under one contract, called *subaccounts*. These variable subaccounts are usually managed by well-known investment managers who clone their mutual fund strategies for the insurance company issuing the contracts. However, they are not, in and of themselves, the actual mutual fund.

These contracts also come in many shapes and sizes, and each company offers its own benefit riders that can be added to the contract for a fee to guarantee certain income payout amounts or death benefit features. With options to invest in the equity markets, these vehicles have the ability to benefit from the long-term growth of stock prices and dividends, but they also offer bond portfolios and fixed interest accounts, making them easier to custom design to your needs.

It's important to note that at your death, in a variable annuity, you are usually guaranteed the market value of the contract or what you invested, whichever is greater at that time. That means if you die while the market value is less than what you invested, your beneficiary will at least get back what you put in, minus any withdrawals. Some companies offer riders for an added fee to guarantee certain amounts of lifetime income payments, as well.

A mutual fund or managed portfolio of stocks cannot offer these types of guarantees, but they do come at an increased cost. The added mortality and expense charges of a variable annuity are basically an insurance premium for providing contract guarantees. These products can be a fit for someone wanting to share with an insurance company some of the risk of outliving their money.

While this is not intended to be a deep dive on annuities, it is important to know what they are and how and when to use them—or not use them—as you develop your wealth accumulation and lifetime income plan. The earnings are not taxed until withdrawn, which can be an attractive feature depending on your situation. And of course, if you already own one or more of these financial products, make sure you understand exactly how they work so you are not surprised when you go to access it at retirement.

So far we've only *discussed* deferred annuities, which are used for accumulation and can be turned into income later, but there are also *immediate* annuities that can be funded with lump-sum deposits and turned into monthly income right away as an important part of your distribution strategy at retirement. In fact, if you get to the doorstep of retirement without ample assets to kick off the income you'll need at a 4.5 percent withdrawal rate, considering a fixed or variable annuitization to put some guarantees around your monthly income can make good sense.

Like any other financial tool in the tool chest, you just want to make sure you are using it the way it was designed to work. So many times, we see good tools applied to the wrong job.

The Importance and Power of Stocks

Remember, you're not planning *to* retirement; you're planning *through* retirement. Your investment time horizon isn't your retirement day. Ideally, it's thirty years or more beyond your retirement day. Having a growing income stream that will provide for you and your spouse that long requires being careful about investing too conservatively. When you're setting aside sums of capital to draw income from five, ten, twenty, or thirty years from now, or perhaps to leave as a legacy, a well-balanced, broadly diversified portfolio of equities is your best defense against outliving your money.

So, why stocks?

In rounded numbers, large company stocks have averaged around a 10 percent total return annually from 1926 through the end of 2021, while long-term government bonds have averaged around 6 percent over that same time period. Treasury bills and inflation have both averaged around 3 percent per year.

But that's only part of the story. When you subtract inflation from those gross returns, you get a roundabout number for the growth in real terms net of inflation. For stocks, you get a 7 percent real return, and for bonds you get about a 3 percent real return. Another way to look at it is that, historically, stocks have produced double or more the real return of bonds. That is to say, you will have earned more than twice the return on your money from *owning* companies through stocks versus *loaning* to them and the government through bonds.

One of the main reasons people give up more than half of the return of stocks to own bonds is that bonds feel safe. You loan a company or the government your money, and they guarantee to give it back to you at some defined point with interest payments along the way. As we've said, over short time periods, this is advisable, but for longer periods of time, that perceived safety starts to cost you both in terms of total return and purchasing power.

Another reason is the fear of volatility. When we feel scared, we are programmed as humans to run first and ask questions later. But we've already established that volatility is not only normal and happens all the time, it is the very fact that stocks can fluctuate in price both up and down that leads to superior returns since the "up years" have beaten the "down years" more frequently and to a greater degree. Volatility can indeed trigger the "flight" instinct, but enduring it has offered great rewards.

Bill was born in August of 1965, when the S&P 500 Index was around eighty-six.[14] That's not a typo—it was just eighty-six. At the end of 2021, that index closed at 4,766, up about 55 times over those fifty-six years. At the beginning of the book, we outlined some of the events that have

---

14   "S&P 500 Historical Prices by Year," accessed March 11, 2022, https://www.multpl.com/s-p-500-historical-prices/table/by-year.

happened over our lifetimes, but from a market perspective, there have been ten bear markets since 1965 (S&P 500 declines of 20 percent or more). Among those were three of the worst periods for stocks in recorded history (1973 to 1974, 2000 to 2002, and 2007 to 2009). Through all of that, the S&P 500 Index compounded annually with dividends reinvested at around 10.4 percent.[15]

Stocks are not some random financial instrument. They represent real ownership in some of the best companies in the world. What goes along with ownership is the right to vote and the right to your share of cash dividends declared by the company's board of directors. How much each company earns per share impacts the price per share and the amount of dividends paid out to shareholders after the board decides how to best deploy the company's earnings.

The reason the collective stocks of the S&P 500 have gone up over time is that the earnings of those companies have gone up over time. Each year, the leaders of this diversified set of companies meet to update their plans for growing their businesses to new heights. They look for new markets, new customers, new products to sell to existing customers, and so on.

---

15   Damodaran Online, "Historical Returns on Stocks, Bonds and Bills: 1928–2021," January 2022, https://pages.stern.nyu.edu/~adamodar/New_Home_Page/datafile/histretSP.html.

STOCK MARKET CYCLES

S&P 500 Index over the past fifty years (Log Scale)

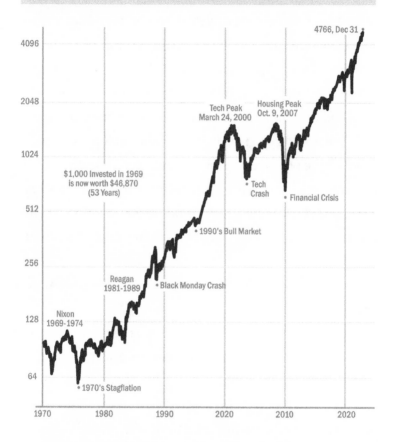

- As this chart shows (log scale), the stock market has performed well over the past fifty years despite short term ups and downs.
- These periods of turbulence were due to economic, political, and global turmoil during those decades.
- This emphasizes the importance of staying invested, rather than focusing on days or months, especially as volatility rises.

Source: Standard and Poor's
© 2022 Cleamomics, Inc.

The main reason the index has grown so much over Bill's lifetime is that corporate earnings are up almost 40 times since then. If you were considering purchasing ownership in any business, whether a popsicle stand or shares of a publicly traded company, one of the first questions you would ask to determine if the asking price is fair is, "How much does it earn, and how much does it net after all expenses are paid?" Then you would pay a reasonable multiple of those earnings based on the type of company and industry it operates in.

Corporate dividends for the S&P 500 are up around 21 times over that same time period, while inflation, represented by the CPI, is up a little less than 9 times.[16] Put that into perspective for a minute. The *income* from the S&P 500 rose over twice as fast as the cost of living. Talk about an inflation hedge!

You needed the income to rise by at least 9 times to afford the same goods and services, and it actually did twice that. While your value was fluctuating from day to day, month to month, and year to year, down at some point every year and more than a third or so every five or six years on average, your dividends made a steady march forward with only a few interruptions.

16 Damodaran Online, "Historical Earnings Changes per Year: S&P 500," accessed March 11, 2022, https://pages.stern.nyu. edu/~adamodar/New_Home_Page/datafile/spearn.htm.

Maybe you're thinking the same thing people say to us sometimes in meetings: "But I don't have fifty-six years left to live. Maybe only thirty or so."

We'll grant you that point, but the story doesn't really change. From the end of 1991 through the end of 2021, the S&P 500 Index went up over 11 times, and not surprisingly, corporate earnings went up a little less than 11 times. The dividends of the index are up around 5 times, and inflation is up just about 2 times over that same period. We see no reason to believe that the next thirty years will be any different.

One of the best ways to make money in equities is to *not get scared* and do the wrong thing at the wrong time. This requires internal fortitude, if not professional reassurance.

You can own shares of stock directly, or through mutual funds or the ETFs that own them, which makes it easier to diversify among different sizes of companies and even different countries, but by all means, you will want to be diversified across different asset classes. Often referred to as asset allocation, how you blend the funds together and rebalance them from time to time is a personal strategy unique to your situation. But *owning* versus *loaning* is the critical variable to patient, long-term wealth accumulation.

AVOIDING BIG MISTAKES

We've seen people build significant wealth by concentrating their holdings, but investors don't usually stay wealthy that way. It's one of the biggest mistakes people make with their money: putting too much on one pony in the race rather than spreading it across many. That's true for assets like stocks, but it's also true in other areas.

During the financial crisis of 2008, many people who were underdiversified in their investments with a lot of real estate holdings got into major trouble. When real estate values crashed suddenly, they owed more than the properties were worth, and they found themselves upside down. Prices eventually recovered (if you remained solvent and held on), but having 100 percent of your money in any one investment for long is usually not a good idea. More recently, many real estate owners got in trouble again during the COVID-19 crisis when rental protections prevented them from collecting rent for more than a year and a half.

There's a reason why we say in this industry, "If you concentrate to accumulate, you have to diversify to protect." Ultimately, there is no "one-size-fits-all" investment portfolio, and each portfolio needs to be designed to meet the needs of the individual. We have some clients who invest only 30 percent of their holdings in stocks and the rest in more conservative things, such as bonds, but we also have clients who invest 90 percent in stocks and keep just 10 percent in cash and bonds. Your plan should dictate your portfolio, not the other way around.

But being underdiversified is only one of the "biggies." We see it with corporate executives who are heavily weighted in their own company's stock, and we see it with business owners, who typically have 80 percent or more of their net worth tied up in their business. As we said, you can build wealth by concentrating, but staying concentrated increases the risk of being like that one single pencil we talked about.

We've found over time that there are a host of common mistakes people make with their money, sometimes two or three at the same time:

- **Being overdiversified**—Having a few eggs in way too many baskets makes it harder to achieve economies of scale and can trick you into thinking you're diversifying, even though many of the baskets are similar.

- **Panicking**—Volatility happens all the time, but it has been temporary. Panicking out of your shares during normal market pullbacks turns temporary declines into permanent losses.

- **Euphoria**—This could also be called "greed" or "irrational exuberance," but it happens as markets rise to peaks and investors excitedly follow the herd and feel that they are missing out.

- **Speculating instead of investing**—Speculating is like gambling for a quick or potential high return, looking at stocks somewhat like casino chips or a roll of the dice. Investing is thinking like the owner of a company, patiently building value and compounding gains over a longer period of time. Both are fine on their own, but be careful not to mistake one for the other.

- **Investing for yield instead of total return**—In the bond market, *yield* is the income a bond pays over time, but *total return* refers to the income, plus capital gains or losses and price appreciation. Always consider an investment from a total return perspective. Chasing the highest yielding investments without paying attention to price swings has caused many investors to experience unexpected losses.

- **Letting the tax-tail wag the dog**—Many people won't sell shares when they should because they want to avoid paying capital gains taxes, only to watch the value crater anyway. Focus on the 80 to 90 percent you keep instead of the 10 to 20 percent you have to pay the tax collector. Taxes are a factor, but hardly the most important factor.

You can see right away how people can make more than one of these mistakes at a time. Euphoria tends to lead to speculation and then underdiversification as people get excited about the latest hot idea, like many did with internet stocks in the spring of 2000 or real estate in 2007.

Individuals have different appetites for volatility, and everyone needs to be able to sleep at night. What we have tried to lay out in this chapter is that patience and belief are crucial components to long-term wealth building. We have also attempted to show the downsides of what most people would call "playing it safe." Hopefully, you can now see why we think of investments that grow and protect your purchasing power as safer than those that erode or destroy your purchasing power over time.

It's counterintuitive, but in a way that makes sense. If it were intuitive, most people would be wealthy and well-prepared for retirement. But most people are, in fact, not wealthy, and most are woefully underprepared for retirement.

That said, there are many online risk assessment questionnaires you can take to help you decide how much tolerance you have for volatility and risk, and we have included one at *www.runwaydecade.com*. Many of these define risk from a principal standpoint, but perhaps now that you know the real long-term risk of purchasing power, you can answer them with a different mindset.

Whatever you have accumulated up to now, whatever you decide about your own comfort level with risk going forward, and whatever tools you use to invest for wealth accumulation, now is the time to take action and make any adjustments to put you in the best possible financial shape for the rest of the ride.

We'll help you do that in the next chapter.

RISK ASSESSMENT TOOL

Investment opportunities exist across a broad spectrum of both risk and reward. Some are high-risk, high-reward, while others are low-risk, low-reward. Use the free tool at *www. runwaydecade.com* to determine how much risk you are comfortable with and willing to undertake.

CREATE YOUR
ACTION CHECKLIST

"The plan is nothing; the planning is everything."
—Dwight D. Eisenhower

t's homework time—time to get tactical! You've done a lot of thinking up to this point and identified the general direction you need to take, and now we're going to identify some specific action steps. If you're like us, when you get three or four thoughts running around in your head at the same time, they start beating up on each other and nothing gets done, so we recommend getting them out of your head and putting all of those thoughts down on paper.

You could also use your computer, digital task list, or app on your phone, if you prefer. Everyone has their own to-do list system, but in our experience, there's something about the act of writing it down by hand that helps get your thoughts in order and makes them stickier. The checklist you create will enable you to start working on your plans one step at a time and give you a sense of accomplishment when you highlight or mark them as complete.

We've included a sample checklist in this chapter, but you can download a full and complete template at *www. runwaydecade.com*.

To determine your first steps, look back at the Financial Matrix in Chapter 5 and some of the questions about what's working and what's not working in Chapter 6, if you need ideas. In the first column, write down the areas that you need to update, change, or improve that you know about and also any areas where you have questions or doubts that need some answers in order to be 100 percent confident. For example, maybe you need to revisit your life insurance terms and beneficiaries, review your 401(k) choices, set up a power of attorney, or create a living will.

You can also start with some low-hanging fruit, those things that are easy to knock out quickly. Making progress

THE ACTION LIST

	What needs to be updated, improved or changed?	Why is it important?	Who needs to be involved?	What is the first action step?	Target Completion Date
1.					
2.					
3.					
4.					
5.					
6.					

right away can be encouraging and energizing. Remember, for some things, there's a moment in time when they're too late to address, so put those near the top and be proactive in knocking them out.

Next, it's important to write down why each area is important to address. Only you can answer that question, but it's your motivation to take action and see it through to completion. As an example, for "set up a power of attorney," you might write, "To help take care of mom if she is unable to make decisions herself." There's usually an emotional button for the answer to each why, whether it's to remove fear, worry, or anxiety, to feel excitement from gaining something, or just to increase your confidence.

You will also want to write down the names of people involved in helping with each area. It could be just you, or you and your spouse or partner, or the name of a professional you work with like a CPA, attorney, insurance agent, or financial advisor. It can also be a good idea to have an accountability partner who will check in to make sure you continue taking action. Think of it like getting fit. It's hard to stick to a fitness regime without some kind of coaching or accountability to keep you on track. Your accountability partner doesn't necessarily have to be a professional. It could be a friend or coworker who wants to go through the process for their own planning at the same time.

As we discussed earlier, people tend to get stuck or procrastinate for many reasons, but one of the main ones is that they don't focus on the very next step they need to take to make progress. Once the cellophane is ripped off the task, the momentum begins. So, for each area you identify, jot down the first action you will take. It could be, "Email Bob to set an appointment," "Go online and print out my account holdings," or "Call my agent and get my policy details." None of these should be big or vague. They should be small, easy, and immediately actionable. This isn't everything that needs to be done, just the very first or very next thing.

Last, give yourself a "due by date" for each area. Set a deadline that isn't too far out—enough time to make progress but not enough to procrastinate. Remember, the deadline is for completion of the project, not for the first action. The first action should be taken within the next twenty-four to forty-eight hours to get the ball rolling, and once that specific action is complete, it could create additional actions, and the process continues until completion of the goal.

As you make progress and check items off your list, you will continue to feel energized and accomplished. It's a bit like cleaning up a messy room. You can see the actual progress in real time and feel inspired to keep going and finish well.

Having a checklist and making regular progress on your action items really does put you in a very elite crowd. You'll be ahead of the game because most people won't ever undertake this type of proactive planning. It's a bit like having the answer sheet to your own personal test.

But right now, this is where the rubber meets the road. This is where real progress is made. You have prepared well and have your plan in hand, but you have come to a crucial fork in the road with really only two choices. Will you take action, or not? The choice is yours.

9

THE ROAD DIVERGES

"Always bear in mind that your resolution to
succeed is more important than any other thing."
—Abraham Lincoln

A long the path to retirement, you will come to a fork in the road. One side leads to confidence, the other to regret. One leaves you feeling successful and thriving, and the other veers off toward fear, disappointment, worry, and doubt. The road to confidence is paved with purposeful action, monitoring, and updating your action checklist as life changes and projected information becomes actual information. The road to regret is paved with fear, inaction, and drifting forward. Success is about acting rather than reacting.

We need look no further than Newton's First Law of Motion for inspiration here: "An object at rest stays at rest and an object in motion stays in motion with the same speed and in the same direction unless acted upon by an unbalanced force." Just because you made a plan and put your things in order to take action doesn't mean you're out of the woods. As Peter Marshall said, "Small deeds done are better than great deeds planned." Plus, by this age, we already have years of experience in learning that we most definitely will be "acted upon by an unbalanced force," right?

A lot of things have happened and could still happen along the way: a health crisis, a hurricane, a job loss, divorce, caring for aging parents, and so on. But those things may happen regardless of whether you are "in motion" or "at rest." If you are in motion, it's easier to stay in motion, acting rather than reacting.

To use our original metaphor, once you're approaching the end of the runway, there's no going back. You can't stop, back up, and try again. Either you take off successfully or you live differently than you had hoped. Or maybe, if you have the energy, you are forced to extend the runway—something actual pilots don't have the luxury of doing!

Getting to retirement age and lamenting about how it just didn't work out like you hoped financially is, in most cases, not really any different than getting to the operating table for a triple bypass and wondering how you got there. You don't get to either place by chance. You behave your way there slowly over time by the actions you take and the decisions you make.

James Clear said in his book *Atomic Habits*, "Every action you take is a vote for the type of person you wish to become." Your actions and decisions during the runway decade could be the most impactful of your life, at least as it pertains to planning for a successful retirement.

It's a big commitment, but remember, you're not doing this for some stranger. You're doing this for your future self and your loved ones. Dr. Hal Hershfield is a psychologist and professor at the UCLA Anderson School of Management and, as his professional bio puts it, he "studies how thinking about time transforms the emotions and alters the judgments and decisions people make. While he was a Ph.D. student at Stanford University, his research concentrated on the psychology of long-term decision-making and how time affects people's lives—specifically at a moment when Americans are living longer and saving less."

He gave a TED Talk on this exact subject, titled "How Can We Help Our Future Selves?" and we highly recommend investing the twelve minutes or so to take this one in. It's available on YouTube or by going to his website at *www.halhershfield.com*, where you will also find other videos he's recorded and articles he has authored on the subject.

In the talk, Hershfield explains that brain science and other studies he's performed suggest that it's likely that you, like most people he studied, do not see your future self as "you." You see that version of yourself more like a stranger when you think about yourself in retirement.

During the studies, scientists first measured participants' brain activity while they looked at current pictures of themselves and talked about themselves. Next they measured the activity while participants talked about and looked at pictures of random people they didn't know, and noted how different parts of the brain reacted. Then, they asked the participants to imagine themselves as being their older future selves and talk about their future plans. The funny thing is, while thinking about their future selves, oddly enough their brain patterns mirrored those from when they were talking about and looking at pictures of strangers.

Since we are hardwired as humans to take care of ourselves first and then those who we are emotionally connected to like family and close friends *before* helping a stranger, you are less willing to do anything for "future you" today if you don't see that person as you. If that's the case, then it's hard to make sacrifices now in order to take care of "future you" because you're treating them as a different person. It's the old "put the oxygen mask on yourself before you help others" thing again, except that that "future you" is still yourself, not an "other." Give that guy or gal some oxygen too!

Hershfield goes on to say that the most successful people when it comes to health and wealth tend to see their future selves as sort of a best friend. They have an emotional connection that makes "today you" take steps now to help "future you." That seventy-year-old person who will reap the rewards of your hard work someday is you, not someone else. It's important to visualize this in your mind, so that you will see the hard work you're doing *now* as benefiting yourself *then*.

As you think about your future self, remember it's okay to be a little bit selfish. Actually, it's more than okay; it's important. According to an article in *Bloomberg* titled "Your Kids are Ruining Your Retirement," many Americans are sacrificing their retirement savings, as well as their ability to save, in order to fund unnecessary expenses for their grown children.[17]

---

17 Carol Hymowitz, "Your Kids Are Ruining Your Retirement," Bloomberg, March 5, 2015, https://www.bloomberg.com/news/articles/2015-03-05/parents-risk-retirement-to-support-millennial-kids.

You're not going to be able to help your children, yourself, causes you care about, or anyone else if you are struggling financially heading into retirement. No one wants to be someone else's financial burden, so you have to see putting the oxygen mask on yourself before you help your adult children as a gift to them as well.

In other words, make sure your own financial plans are in order, and do what you have to do to keep them protected. If you want to give to your adult children out of the excess that is left over, that's perfectly fine, but don't sacrifice your own future to help other people who are capable of helping themselves. Maintaining health and wealth for yourself will be the gift that keeps giving to everyone in your life.

PUT ONE FOOT IN FRONT OF THE OTHER

How do you create health and wealth? A little bit at a time. Little steps of progress on your action list take what are seemingly large, far-off goals and break them down into pieces that can be more easily handled and managed. Remember the Rankin/Bass 1970 Christmas special *Santa Claus is Coming to Town*? In an effort to help the Winter Warlock change his mean and ugly ways and become a nice person, Kris Kringle suggests he needs to take that first step as he sings, "Put One Foot in Front of the Other."

We apologize in advance if you hum this in your head for the rest of the day! In one verse, he sings:

If you want to change your direction
If your time of life is at hand
Well don't be the rule, be the exception
A good way to start is to stand.

And that's how you'll achieve your retirement goals, no matter where you are starting from today: simply put one foot in front of the other on your action list. It's how you'll stop money from leaking out, build up your savings, generate wealth through investments, and create an income stream to last throughout your retirement years. Slowly, over time, take action to create, implement, monitor, and adjust your plans.

Whether you have a simple or complex estate, the individual action you have to take should be fairly simple to get done. Or, as we like to say, "simple but not easy." The "not easy" part is maintaining the discipline, willpower, and commitment to *keep* taking action when you get stuck or don't know which way to turn. Getting to a point of confidence is great, but confidence is not a permanent state. Our mentor and veteran advisor Nick Murray says it's like vitamin C: the body doesn't store it indefinitely, so you have to continually replenish it.

You may be confidently taking action today, but what will you do if there's a big market downturn next week and your investment portfolio loses some value? What will you do if you experience a health crisis? Suddenly, your confidence will be shaken. When that happens, it's important to come back to your plan and make adjustments as needed, so that you can restore whatever sense of direction and confidence you have temporarily lost. Yes, you are referring back to your plan, but it's all in an effort to make progress forward toward your goals.

As the writer Donna Schultz put it, "At one time or another, we all stand at the crossroads and at the fork in the road. We can go back where it's comfortable, predictable, and easy. Or we can go forward. If you go back, my friend, you will miss the ride of your life!"

That's where you're at right now. Confidence begins with a commitment to take the path of action. It's the reason it's so important to state "why" an action is important to you because that is the focus of your commitment. You can't go back in time, of course, but you can certainly spin your wheels, or even lose traction toward your goals if you let inertia set back in.

Many people worry about how other people their age are doing, so they can tell themselves they are either behind or ahead. Sometimes you will run across magazines or websites that suggest that you should have "X" amount of retirement savings by a certain age, say fifty or fifty-five. Whether you look at those and feel good or you look and feel bad about where you stand, all you're looking at is theory and not facts. And certainly not any facts about you and your family.

It doesn't matter how your progress lines up with the statistics, or your neighbor, the guy down the hall at work, or anyone else. All that matters is whether you are on the right path and on track toward *your own* retirement goals in a way that will get you where you want to be by your retirement date. That's it. That's the only game you're playing—your own!

If you've gotten this far, and you've created your action checklist, you're way ahead of the game if you do seek out professional help for pieces of it. Whether you tackle the checklist by yourself or hire a financial advisor to help you think through some of it, you will already be prepared for the first conversation that most will have with you about your goals and dreams and important things you need to do to feel confident. But whether you seek help or not, it's never a good idea to take your hands off the wheel.

When pilots put their planes on autopilot, they don't leave the cockpit to mix and mingle with the passengers, leaving no one at the controls. They engage it to reduce the amount of constant workload on them in an effort to lessen their fatigue and reduce human errors during long flights. But they do so fully aware that if something goes wrong, or they face an unexpected problem, they might have to take over the controls again. For that reason, the pilot and the rest of the flight crew constantly monitor what's going on. Likewise, expect that you will have to make some adjustments along the way.

In the same way, there are plenty of ways for your investments to be running on autopilot, quietly but consistently building wealth for you over the years. However, we have encountered situations where no one was paying attention, and it led to ignoring warning signs that ultimately ended up costing them a lot of money (or money leaking out). Confidence can turn into overconfidence and then complacency.

By monitoring your accounts on a regular basis, you will be ready in case something arises, and you have to take over the controls for a bit and maybe even adjust your course. The same goes for every part of your overall financial and retirement plans.

Recall the exercise we recommended at the beginning of the book: visualize your retirement party and think about what your life is going to be at that time. You've made a lot of progress since we first discussed it and have done some deep thinking about what you really want. You've now clarified the steps it will take to get you there, created an action checklist, and hopefully, you have some sort of accountability partner for making sure you keep the ball moving forward. You are setting yourself up to be the hero of this story.

As you think back on that visioning exercise, all the effort you have made and will make in the years ahead is about the three Ps: Providing, Protecting, and Prospering for those people in your life who are counting on you, including future you. If you and the people in that room the night of your retirement party feel those things, all of the hard work and effort will be worth it.

Keep reminding yourself of that fact and even write those three words down somewhere that you can see them on a regular basis. The delayed gratification, constant monitoring, adjusting, and overcoming your own emotions are all going to be worth it, with you riding in as the hero for those you care about most.

In the end, what separates successful retirees from all others is that they planned for their success. It was an intentional act that demanded sacrifice, discipline, effort, willpower, long-term commitment, and smart decision-making over many years. In fact, successful people in all walks of life tend to do three very simple things that others could do but just don't: (1) they seek advice, (2) they make a plan, and (3) they take action on the plan.

Simple, but as we said before, not easy. If you want to achieve a happy, successful, and financially free future, you have to intentionally plan for and work toward it. There's no other way.

As Yogi Berra said, "When you come to a fork in the road, take it." Effort and lack of effort both produce results, but only one is going to produce results that leave you feeling confident, successful, and thriving. Fortunately, you don't have to do this all by yourself. You can tap into the experience of a trusted advisor who has already gone down the retirement path hundreds, maybe thousands, of times.

THE VALUE AND PRICE OF ADVICE (OR GOING IT ALONE)

"Along the journey, we experience joys, sorrows,
and if we are lucky, a few trusted guides."

—B. Barton

Boeing's entry into the US Army Air Corps' 1935 design competition was called the Model 299, though it would later receive the designation B-17. The plane would play a major role in the battle for air superiority during World War II, but its debut was fairly inauspicious.

The demonstration flight took place on October 30, 1935, at Wright Field near Riverside, Ohio.

As Army Air Corps officers looked on, test pilot Major Ployer Peter Hill guided the plane onto the runway. The Model 299 took off and began a smooth climb. Suddenly, without warning, it stalled, crashed, and burst into flames. The crash killed the pilot and a Boeing employee, and destroyed the prototype airplane.

Later investigation would reveal that the pilot had failed to disengage the wind-gust locks, which keep the plane stable on the ground. In preparing for takeoff, he had simply forgotten a step, and no one else in the cockpit had reminded him. The result was catastrophic. Headlines the next day proclaimed that the Model 299 was "Too Much Plane for One Man to Fly."[18]

The thing is, the Boeing aircraft was superior to the other one being tested that day, and it was a foregone conclusion that they would be awarded the contract. But it ended so poorly that they couldn't be. Perhaps it was a case of overconfidence by the pilot, or the added complexity of a more modern piece of machinery, but it wasn't the quality of the

---

18   Michael R. Gruninger, Markus Kohler, and Captain Giancarlo Buono, "Too Much Plane for One Man to Fly," BART Safety Sense, February–April 2010, https://gcs-safety.com/wp-content/uploads/2020/12/Safety-Sense-BART-n.-125.pdf.

vehicle that forced it to crash. As with so many accidents, it was due to pilot error.

We share this story for one simple reason: as more and more complexity creeps in over time, it's possible that your financial situation will outgrow your ability to figure it all out by yourself. Sometimes, it's too much "plan" for one person to fly. As you approach your action checklist, given the body of knowledge required to properly weigh your options and make sound decisions, you might feel uncomfortable taking on all of these complicated tasks by yourself. You'd be right to be concerned because the stakes are high, and even just a single mistake with your money can change your trajectory at this stage of the game. So many times, the mistakes we see are behavioral and 100 percent "pilot error."

Maybe you're not even the one with the concerns. Maybe it's your spouse, who has begun to question whether you can get all of this done on your own or is worried that your worrying over it will impact your happiness as you approach retirement. Even if you have been handling it all by yourself up to now, and can still handle it going forward, do you really want to have to constantly think about your finances while you're gardening, mowing the yard, on vacation, or fishing?

Wouldn't it be nice if someone else was taking care of the ongoing monitoring for you and just keeping you in the loop? Wouldn't it be nice if someone would take the burden of keeping you on track? As one of our clients put it in their first meeting with us, "Managing our financial picture has become a job, and it's not a job I ever really wanted."

In just about every industry, there is a do-it-yourself option, and flying is no different. You could theoretically pay for flying lessons and learn to fly your own plane. It would take a long time, and you might discover that becoming a pilot is a lot harder than you expected or that you just don't have the mental makeup for it. Alternatively, you could simply and easily buy a ticket on one of the major airlines and ride first class, business coach, or economy, depending on the experience you want. Or you could just go private, have the plane to yourself, hire a pilot, and let them do the flying and handle all the other details for you. The level of service, experience, flight time, and cost would certainly vary, but you'd still get to your destination. The difference in your choices would be the time, temperament, and resources you are willing and able to put into getting what you want or need.

IT'S NOT AS EASY AS IT LOOKS

Some in the media make it sound like planning for retirement is easy and that it would be ridiculous to pay for financial advice when there is so much information out there for free on the web. Creating a will and power of attorney documents, deciding when to claim Social Security, managing an investment portfolio, maximizing savings earnings, learning financial discipline, planning for long-term health care—it's all very easy, or so they would have you believe. Some of it might be simple, and some of it is certainly complex, but blending it all together into a plan specific to your situation is *never* easy.

Yes, you can take care of all of these things yourself. Do your research, figure it out, and handle every step on your own. If you are capable of doing that, we agree that it would be silly to pay someone else to do it for you. However, if you are not 100 percent confident you've got your arms around it, we recommend that you consider getting help.

Even if you decide to go it alone, at the very least, you can get someone with expertise to check your math or double-check your thinking. That way you at least allow for a margin of error and your own human mistakes. Someone once asked us rhetorically, "Do you know how much more money I would have if I'd had someone around to talk me out of all the dumb things I've done with my money over the years?"

Remember the "unknown negatives" from earlier? It can pay to know what you don't know, especially between now and retirement. It's not about who is smarter, it's about acknowledging that we all have blind spots where we need someone with a different perspective to see what we simply cannot.

The deeper you go into your retirement plans, the more complex they're going to get, especially given the ever-changing tax laws, Social Security and Medicare rules, and financial markets. Keeping up with everything on the matrix will inevitably become a big time commitment and as we discussed earlier, human nature being what it is, most people's own behavior causes them to do the wrong thing at the wrong time. Is that a job you really want? Would it be better to let someone else shoulder some of the burden so you can focus on your many other responsibilities? Only you can answer those questions.

But think of it this way. You can change the oil in your car by yourself. It doesn't take long, and you probably have all the tools you need. However, it is messy and complicated, and it's really not that fun to do it yourself, especially if something goes wrong. That's why most people drive to the nearest five-minute oil change place and pay a professional to do it for them while they multitask. Your time is valuable, and it just makes sense to give the job to someone who has changed vehicle oil hundreds or thousands of times.

Likewise, a Certified Financial Planner™ with a thirty-year career has seen thousands of situations and acquired a vast body of knowledge that you can tap into and leverage. Pete often tells a story of going whitewater rafting in Colorado for the first time with his family. Going it alone could have been a disaster, but the guide had been down that mountain stream hundreds of times and knew the exact location of every rock and waterfall to prepare everyone for what was up ahead.

The bottom line is, whatever way you choose to approach this will come with a cost. The idea is to arrive happily and safely at your destination without worry or unacceptable tradeoffs of time, money, purpose, or relationships.

In terms of retirement, it's only going to get harder to keep up with everything as you get older. You may be on top of your game now, but cognitive decline is a reality that most people have to face if they live long enough. We have faced it with clients, and even in our own family, and maybe you have in yours, as well. As one of our clients put it, "I feel like I am smart enough to keep up with this stuff right now, but I need someone I can trust for my family if I'm not around and when I am older and not as sharp." Admitting to yourself that you want or need help is not a weakness, it's a strength.

Sticking with our travel metaphors, let's imagine you set sail on a boat from Boston Harbor to Lisbon, Portugal. You can't just point the boat in the right direction then go below deck and play cards for the rest of the trip, expecting to get to your destination. If it's not going to be you, someone has to pilot the ship and make occasional adjustments to compensate for wind, currents, and other factors.

You may still have a lot of nautical miles to go between your fifties and your eventual retirement age, and adjustments will have to be made from time to time to deal with the unexpected. If you have a co-pilot, you also have shared responsibility. If you go it alone, you own every result 100 percent, good, bad, or ugly, but you can proudly sing Chris Stapleton's hit "Nobody to Blame But Me" at the top of your lungs!

WAYS AN ADVISOR ADDS VALUE

The specific ways that working with an advisor will create value for you will be very personal to your situation and which parts of the matrix you need help with. But there are some common areas that most people can benefit from, and they are mainly behavioral since emotions rule the day when it comes to financial and retirement planning. Here are a few examples:

Building the Roadmap

Even though people who create a vision, establish specific goals, write them down, and measure their progress with an accountability partner achieve greater success by orders of magnitude than those who do not plan at all,[19] the reality is that in our experience most people will never undertake this exercise of deciding on and focusing on what they want.

The way an advisor adds value is by taking you through a deep discussion and dialogue about your past and future and helping you identify and focus on what you really want to achieve or accomplish with your life and for your family or business. Serving as an ongoing thinking partner for your success, an advisor offers behavioral coaching and mentoring along the way to counter the powerful forces of fear, worry, panic, aggressiveness, and overconfidence.

Laying the Track

How do you take big far-off goals and break them down into the routine habits that will help you achieve them? Inch by inch, it's a cinch. Mile by mile, it's a trial.

---

19   Gail Matthews, "The Effectiveness of Four Coaching Techniques in Enhancing Goal Achievement: Writing Goals, Formulating Action Steps, Making a Commitment, and Accountability" (presented at the 9th Annual International Conference on Psychology, Athens, Greece, May 25–28, 2015).

An advisor takes your big goals and breaks them down into manageable steps, and then keeps their finger on the pulse of how well that plan is working, adjusting it as needed. There are a great variety of worthy goals you may communicate to an advisor, whether eliminating some concern or issue, or accomplishing something very positive.

Regardless of the type, an advisor can break it down into steps that can be knocked out in the right order, making calculations, projections, plans, and checkpoints to work toward the goals you say are important to you.

Planning and Managing Investments

Who will stand between you and the common mistakes that many investors make on their own without professional guidance? Asset allocation and rebalancing, asset location, active tax-loss harvesting, and controlling investment expenses all add to an investor's bottom line return, and all provide a fraction of value to behavioral coaching. Left to our own vices, we are subject to the human emotions of euphoria and panic at the exact wrong times during market cycles. People become overconfident and underdiversified at the top of a market, and fearful and frozen at market bottoms.

Through a disciplined process of investment selection, rebalancing, and ongoing management of investor behavior, an advisor could help you create organized and diversified portfolios and then serve as a buffer between you and the myriad dysfunctional decisions and mindsets that may creep in around your money. Just by showing you the big mistakes investors make, an advisor could help you avoid them and the impact they may have on your portfolio.

Managing and Minimizing Taxes

Every year, there are millions of dollars left on the table by American taxpayers simply from not taking advantage of all that the tax code offers them in the way of deductions, credits, and other strategies.

An advisor should be looking at your situation holistically, mining for dollars you are needlessly leaving on the table. They should look at your past few years' tax returns from a financial planning perspective to look for opportunities you can capitalize on.

Managing Inherent Risks

Life will happen. That is a given. Family breadwinners, business partners, and other key people die every single day. Knowing that you and your family are adequately protected in the event of an unexpected loss of health, life, income, property, or even their ability to live independently is a major source of confidence.

The same goes for your business continuing uninterrupted financially if an owner, partner, or key employee dies. Quite literally, every single day people become uninsurable, or at the very least life and disability insurance become more expensive than they were before. Most people don't have enough life insurance, and many have none at all, leaving their families in a financial lurch if the breadwinner dies or becomes disabled. Even fewer are protected against a sustained need for long-term care.

An advisor may be able to add value by looking not only at the asset side of the Balance Sheet, but also the liability side. When considering the liability side, the inherent risks of loss are evaluated and then shared with companies who insure those risks. Analyzing and evaluating current risk management programs and making sure they are still relevant and adequate is crucial to building a solid financial foundation.

Budgeting and Cash Flow

What gets measured gets managed. What gets measured and managed improves. Having a budget increases the chances of building wealth over time. Most people never budget or have a loose version of it in their heads. Many are not saving well enough to be prepared for a financial emergency, much less saving for college or retirement.

An advisor might be useful in helping you get your arms around your inflows and outflows so you can identify areas to cut expenses and increase savings and investments. Plugging small leaks can add up to a lot of money over time that could be used to knock out other important financial goals.

Organizing, Monitoring, and Guiding Your Financial Life

Most people are unorganized, have multiple scattered parts to their financial life, and have trouble getting and keeping their arms around it all. Have you ever stopped to put a price on what disorganization might be costing you? People who are organized make fewer mistakes, save more, capitalize on opportunities faster, and adjust faster if something bad happens.

Working with an advisor might also eliminate the anxiety of financial disorganization and lack of financial awareness, replacing worry and anxiety with systems, processes, check-ins, and ultimately confidence about your entire life and not just about your money.

Planning for Confident Retirement

Do you know what it will cost you to retire, not just the day you do, but ten, twenty, or thirty years later? Many people never save outside of what Social Security or their employer might provide.

An advisor could help you plan ahead and then measure your progress on a continual basis so that you remain confident about what your lifestyle will be like once you stop working. They ask you the right questions to help you determine the lifestyle you want in retirement and then help you make progress toward it by monitoring and adjusting as needed.

Leaving a Legacy and Transitioning Your Wealth

Assuming you have planned well for your own needs, are there other people and/or causes that you care deeply about that, if possible, you could leave a meaningful legacy to beyond your life? If you don't specify how you want things handled and distributed at your death, you might leave messes for those who are left behind to have to figure it out.

An advisor may be able to serve as an accountability partner to help you stop and consider how you want to pass on your assets and your values, and then align you with the appropriate legal and tax professionals to help you document and communicate your wishes.

Life Transitions and Taking Care of Others

Do you have an ongoing thinking partner to help you think through the financial implications of life's various transitions, both good and not so good? Life happens. We age, relationships change, jobs change, or we might receive a sudden inheritance or windfall of some kind. Without someone you like and trust who you know understands your situation, you are prone to costly mistakes when left to your own devices, making decisions based on emotion instead of logic.

An advisor helps you think through the financial implications of any change and gives you a sounding board for your emotions and behavior so you can make informed decisions.

EVERY ADVISOR IS DIFFERENT

Beyond how advisors *could* add value, it's important to determine what ways they are *capable* of adding value, or how they *will* add value. In other words, someone you think of as an advisor may just be an investment product specialist or an insurance agent. Some are brokers, registered investment advisors, financial life planners, or maybe even bankers or accountants. The titles and services provided can be varied and confusing, but above all, it should be someone with experience, competency, professional credentials, professional references, and someone who you like and trust.

We also strongly recommend that you find a group or advisor with a proven process, reliable systems, and a talented team around them who can help along the way.

Many advisors are great at initiating relationships but fall off when it comes to servicing them. Getting good advice is expected, but friendly, courteous, professional, proactive support is even harder to find and becomes priceless over time.

As different as advisors are in name and services, their compensation models are also all over the map. Some bill by the hour, some by retainer, some are compensated by commissions on the products you purchase, and others only charge quarterly advisory fees on the assets they manage. We've seen models that charge a percentage of income or a percentage of net worth, some that are flat-rate dollar amounts, and so on.

Debates go on in the financial services industry all the time about the best model, but it really comes down to the value the advisor intends to deliver to you and what they charge for that value. As the old saying goes, "Price is only an issue to the extent that it exceeds value." That's another way of saying make sure you get what you pay for, which requires knowing what you are paying, how you are paying, and what you can expect to receive for what you pay. Transparency in these areas is vital to determining the true value.

In our opinion, it's perfectly fine to have multiple advisors with different disciplines (insurance, investment, tax, legal, etc.), but you can only have one plan that everyone works off of and communicates about. Each advisor can't have their own uncoordinated plan for you, your family, or your business. You have one life, and it needs one plan. If you've never brought all of your existing advisors together, doing so while you are on the runway is a really good idea.

For this very reason, we use a retainer fee process we call The Confident Wealth Experience®, and one of the steps in that process, called The Advisor Link Advantage, makes sure everyone is singing off the same choir page, so to speak. The entire process is a holistic approach that takes a 360-degree look at your overall financial picture.

Unlike many in the industry, we have separated fees for planning and advice from fees for implementing the advice. That creates the flexibility for clients to engage with us in three flexible ways: (1) for planning and advice services only, (2) for implementation services only, or (3) for both together from start to finish.

The important thing is that you ask the right questions and interview at least a few potential vetted options. If you are approached out of the blue with a can't-miss offer or a high-pressure salesperson, that's probably a sign that the person is trying to sell something to you whether you need it or not.

THE CONFIDENT WEALTH EXPERIENCE

THE CONFIDENT CARE SYSTEM
Guidance for Navigating an Unpredictable Future

THE DISCOVERY CONVERSATION
Discovering Your Past and Envisioning Your Future

THE CONFIDENT WEALTH MONITOR
Keeping Our Hands on the Wheel

YOUR CONFIDENT WEALTH STRATEGIES
Your Roadmap to Success

THE ADVISOR LINK ADVANTAGE
Coordinating a Treasure Trove of Experts to Support You

YOUR CONFIDENT WEALTH ACTION PLAN
Putting Your Plan in Motion

THE DISCOVERY CONVERSATION

- Identify what is important to you and what you want to change, improve, or develop in the future
- Inventory your assets, liabilities, benefits, income sources, and expenses
- Determine areas where we can add value, discuss how to engage with us, and review our services levels

YOUR CONFIDENT WEALTH STRATEGIES

- A written assessment of your existing holdings and strategies to identify strengths and weaknesses
- Detailed analysis of retirement income planning, education savings, risk management, asset allocation, tax efficiency, cash flow, and estate planning
- Benchmark where you are compared to where you want and need to be and perform a gap analysis

YOUR CONFIDENT WEALTH ACTION PLAN

- Specific investment recommendations and financial strategies based on your plan
- An individualized checklist and timeline to help support your progress
- Establish new accounts, fill in insurance gaps, restructure liabilities, and take other actions as needed

THE ADVISOR LINK ADVANTAGE

- Referrals to other trusted resources to help implement parts of your plan as needed or work within your existing advisory team
- Accounting, legal, insurance, pension administration, banking, and mortgage
- Business and entrepreneurial coaching

THE CONFIDENT WEALTH MONITOR

- Investment portfolio and wealth strategy reviews at regular intervals
- Your Confident Wealth Hub: a web-based system that gives you a daily updated single view of your financial life
- Goal progress monitoring to keep you on track and adjust as needed

THE CONFIDENT CARE SYSTEM

- Regular communication via calls, meetings and electronic messages with timely response to all inquiries
- Assistance with navigating the financial implications of life's various transitions
- The Opportunity Evaluator: perspectives, processes, shortcuts, timesavers, thinking templates, and leadership for tackling your future needs

A holistic planner is probably going to be a lot more helpful in more areas than a specialist who focuses only on specific products or sales tactics. If you show up to an advisor's office, and the first thing they say is, "Let's have a look at your statements and see what your investment portfolio looks like," it's a good sign that they are really only interested in your money and not your whole financial plan. That's fine and dandy if you know going in that it's just about investing, but even then, the types of questions they ask you will tell you whether they are there to help or whether they see you solely as the owner of a certain sum of money.

Now you may be thinking, "Yes, but financial coaches and advisors charge fees!" That is true, but instead of focusing only on the cost, focus on the value a quality advisor can deliver that you may not be able to get alone. First off, if they can prevent you from making even one of the big mistakes we mentioned in Chapter 7, they may save you an untold multiple of their annual fee. And many people make more than one of those mistakes over their lifetime. That's your premium for "Big Mistake Insurance," in a sense.

As the quotable former Notre Dame football coach Lou Holtz once said, "You don't need the big plays to win; you just have to eliminate the dumb ones." We're not saying any person is dumb, but some financial moves certainly turn out to be. A proactive advisor can help you think through things in the right way to avoid a costly mistake, and just like we said about life insurance, the cost of the solution is usually a fraction of the cost of the problem—and likewise for the cost of a good advisor. As Ben Franklin famously said, "An ounce of prevention is worth a pound of cure."

Additionally, an advisor might even help you make some wise decisions that help boost your return over time by more than what they charge you by helping you select more appropriate investment choices, in addition to rebalancing and adjusting as needed. Sure, this is a big unknown with no guarantees as you begin a relationship, but it could and should also make a big difference over your investing lifetime.

Last, but certainly not least, do you think it's possible that working with an advisor and their team could save you the equivalent of their fee in time, worry, and record-keeping so you can focus on things that are more important to you? What would that be worth to you?

Don't look at the fee in a vacuum. Consider the value you get in return. As always, beauty is in the eye of the beholder. A good coach or advisor can do the one thing you cannot do yourself: hold a mirror up and show you what things look like from the outside. As we said, you can't read the label from inside the jar, and sometimes it pays to have a co-pilot or an outside set of eyes looking in.

CONCLUSION

If you're in your fifties, the clock is ticking, but there's still time to work toward a better retirement for yourself and your spouse or partner. What do you want your life to look like in twelve to fifteen years? What quality of life do you hope for once you need to stop working or work just becomes optional?

Right now, you can begin to make progress toward that retirement lifestyle you envision. Don't put it off any longer. Living in regret over past financial mistakes won't fix anything. Sometimes, clients walk through our door full of regret over losses from bad investments, trusting the wrong so-called "experts," or not setting aside enough money throughout their careers. But that's all water under the bridge. Now is the time for action.

When people fill us in on their details and lament about the past, we tell them, "That's not who you *are*. That's who you were. Who you are now will be defined by what you do going forward. Pull the useful lessons and learning from your past experiences forward but leave the rest of it behind."

Even if your past isn't full of mistakes, if you've arrived in your fifties having made a lot of good choices about your finances, you have to be careful of overconfidence and complacency. You're on the runway now, and every decision or indecision gets magnified as the runway gets shorter and shorter. Never leave your financial plans on autopilot as you approach takeoff.

Maybe you've procrastinated because the prospect of organizing every part of your financial plans feels overwhelming. Fear is the enemy of planning, but hopefully the thinking process we've given you in this book will help you make progress. Clarify your vision for retirement, determine your flight path for getting there, and create an action checklist of things that need to be done. Begin working your way through the action checklist, starting with those items that need the most immediate attention.

When you do this, you will build confidence, and the fear will just melt away. It has been said that fear is the only thing that gets smaller as you run toward it.

RECAPPING THE PROCESS

- Decide what you want in vivid detail.
- Identify the obstacles and challenges.
- Pinpoint your current situation/location.
- Mind your health, as well.
- Take the big-picture view, not just your assets.
- Figure out what's working and what's not.
- Determine the best vehicles to take you there.
- Make your action list.
- The road splits to confidence or regret, so choose your path wisely!
- Go it alone or decide to use a guide.

But you have to get started. The runway's not as long as it looks from the sidelines, and the plane moves fast as it approaches takeoff. Recently, we had a conversation with our father, who is eighty-two years old, and he said, "The calendar flips so quickly now. When you're five years old, a year is 20 percent of your life, and it seems to take forever. But when you're eighty-two, a single year is about 1.2 percent of your life, and it just flashes by like the fraction that it is."

At fifty years old, a single year is 2 percent of your life, so why not dedicate the next 2 percent of your life to getting the next 40 percent of your life in order? Yes, you have a lot of other things going on to worry about, but you'll never regret setting aside some time now to create a better retirement lifestyle for future you.

Anything that is worth doing is worth doing well. We thought about writing this book for a long time before we actually did it. It wasn't easy to make progress, especially when we have a business to run and families of our own to take care of. Finally, we just had to set aside the time, hire some professional help to accelerate our progress, and get it done. And even then, without the constant guidance, coaching, and nudging, it would honestly have never happened. But you're now holding the fruits of that hard work and of that coaching.

If you're overwhelmed at the thought of getting your finances in order or just the details of making your final approach, don't be afraid to seek professional help. An experienced guide will accelerate your progress and help you get on track faster, and with greater confidence.

The goal of this book wasn't to give you specific investment advice but instead to provide a big-picture overview to get you moving in the right direction. Our goal is really to just help as many people of our era as we can get motivated to stop the drifting and take action. Ultimately, you have to create an action checklist that is right for you, and there will be nuances to it that are unique to your situation. Your retirement plan is your own. It doesn't have to look like anyone else's. As long as it moves you toward your vision of retirement in a healthy way, then it's right for you. It's your story after all and you get to write it the way you want to.

You should now have a good idea of what you need to be thinking about, as well as a process for taking action, building toward retirement, and then monitoring your money as you go forward. If you can wake up each day during your fifties and make just a little bit of progress in your health and wealth, you will reap the rewards for many years to come. Timing is everything, so get started as soon as you finish reading this book by heading over to *www.runwaydecade.com* to download your worksheets. Your best retirement is waiting for you!

ADDITIONAL RESOURCES

For additional resources to help you plan for retirement, create your action checklist, and begin taking action, check out our website at *RunwayDecade.com*. We have a podcast dedicated to financial planning that can help you with all aspects of retirement, along with templates, deep dives, and helpful guides. And it's all complimentary!

BILL'S ACKNOWLEDGMENTS

I have to start by thanking my family. My wife, Melissa, is always supportive in every seemingly wild endeavor I attempt. So, when I told her, "Hey, Pete and I are writing a book," she wasn't shocked at all, just very accommodating of the juggled schedules and impromptu writing retreats. Her support, love, and encouragement throughout this project have been immense, unwavering, and much appreciated.

My daughters, Molly and Miranda, are a constant source of joy and entertainment, and they are two of the smartest people on the planet. I thank them for the laughs, the hugs, and the "love you" that ends nearly every encounter.

I'm grateful to my mom, dad, and many siblings. My dad set a great example of how to work hard and provide. My mom always inspired me to do my best and use my creativity to its fullest. At seventy-nine, *she* became a published author...what an example! Growing up in a house of six children who were all smart and possessed unique talents instilled a drive in each of us. Growing up next to wonderful people makes you want to be wonderful, too. Thanks to my siblings' lifelong support that has led to this moment.

There would be no *The Runway Decade* book without brother Pete. I appreciate his faith in me and my ideas. When he first heard about my runway concept, he said, "That's something. Let's do it." Pete's knowledge and experience certainly form the backbone of the book. I'm grateful to have worked hand-in-hand with him on this project, and in a larger sense, I'm grateful to be working with him in an environment that fosters, honors, and values out-of-the-box, creative thinking. That's rare air in our industry, and it's by Pete's design. Because of that, I feel there is much blank canvas left to paint at Horizon Financial Group.

One of the sheer joys of joining Horizon and changing careers at age fifty (the first year of the runway decade, no less) has been working closely with my youngest brother, Andy. Brothers, not twins. Andy and I work side-by-side in leading the Retirement Plans Division of Horizon. He's one of the most caring people you'll ever meet, and he has been a great example to me on how to interact with clients.

I appreciate his support, his candor, and, most importantly, his quality humor.

I'm thankful to all the other partners and team members at Horizon Financial Group who really got behind the idea of this book and have supported it, each in their own way. Clint, Brooke, Colby, Rebecca, Jennifer, Brookelynn, and Chad, I thank you all!

To Dr. Davey Prout: Nice going on that heart diagnosis and stent placement, man. It would've been hard to write this book otherwise.

To all the mentors, teachers, coaches, teammates, collaborators, directors, staff members, and co-workers I've encountered throughout the years who have impacted me, I thank you. Encouragement and kind words go a long way. There are too many to name, but here are a few that provided ample and instilled confidence: Steve S., Ron, Beau, Suzie, Kevin, Denise, Kemp, Ross, Tom, Ellene, Jacques, Bill, and Clint. I'm told there's still ink left, so also...Pete and Andy.

PETE'S ACKNOWLEDGMENTS

Without the love, support, and constant encouragement from Kelli, my wife and partner in life, I wouldn't have had the space or time necessary to take on something as ambitious as writing a book. I'd need to write another book to list *all* the reasons I am grateful for our relationship, our friendship, and her presence in my life, but as it pertains to this particular effort, I am thankful that she endures my various crazy projects and just lets me be me.

For my children, Shelbi, Jacob, and Taylor, you each inspire me in your own unique ways, and I love all the laughs and experiences we share. I am so far from being a perfect parent, but collectively you've made me strive to try to be one. If anything, I hope this book inspires you to write your own one day, even if it's just for you.

While some people tell me they could never work with family, I find it to be an incredible blessing to work with my brothers, Andy and Bill. Andy is a go-to resource for retirement plans and has been instrumental as one of my sounding boards and partners in growing our firm, Horizon Financial Group, over these many years. I treasure his trust and commitment to always doing the right thing. Plus, he knows I'll tell Mom if he doesn't. :)

Brother Bill, as I like to call him, has been creating things his entire life with a vivid imagination and great sense of humor coupled with a high level of intelligence. In 2015, after consulting with us on a few projects, he took a huge leap of faith, moved his family over two hours away, and brought that creativity full time to our team in Baton Rouge. I'm grateful for that trust and for the chance to laugh, work, and create together. When he approached me with the idea for this book, I knew right away we had to do it, and it has become the latest in a long line of successes from "putting our heads together" on an idea.

To Mom and Dad, I'm not sure how you did it with six kids, but you always encouraged us and told us we could be anything we wanted to be. Thanks for the millions of times you've told us you love us and that you are proud of us. Like most kids, that's all we ever really wanted or needed.

While I'm certain I'd be doing something productive with my life regardless, I know in my heart that Horizon would simply not exist, much less prosper like it has, without my long-term friendship and partnership with Brooke Gautreau. Her unwavering belief in me, her voice of reason, and the level of care that she has brought to our clients and team have made her an invaluable thinking partner and the truest of friends. What a journey it has been over these past two decades, and what wonderful, memorable experiences we have been fortunate enough to share along the way. I know the best is yet to come!

Similarly, without the hard work, dedication, tireless work ethic, and commitment to me and our team that my partner Colby Cypriano has brought to her work over these past fifteen-plus years, our Horizon Advisor Network would be a fraction of its size, if it existed at all. She works at a pace that few can, and she has created an immense amount of leverage for me to be able to focus on growing the firm and taking on projects like this book.

Ditto for my partner Clint Gautreau, who oversees the financial planning and investment management aspects of our business. His well-researched perspectives and analytical abilities have made our entire team better and expanded the ways that we help our clients and affiliated advisors.

For the rest of our Horizon team, in so many ways big and small, Rebecca, Chad, Jennifer, and Brookelynn make us better with their gifts and talents that support each other and our clients. Brookelynn's creative skills helped us lay out the graphics for this book and allowed us to create all of our deliverables in-house, a rare skillset in a financial advisory firm.

I'm grateful for the many clients who have trusted us to guide them on their financial planning and investment matters. Much of the material presented in this book is the direct result of learning from thousands upon thousands of conversations with clients and their families over the past thirty years. We remain humbled and honored that you have chosen us as your guide. Ditto for the many financial advisor friends and collaborators I have encountered along the way, both at Cetera and otherwise. I have learned so much from their willingness to share their wisdom, knowledge, and best practices.

While so many things have changed and so many people have come and gone in my professional life at the corporate level of the industry, my relationship with Brett Harrison has been the one shining exception. We have grown in this business and on this journey together, not just as colleagues, but as friends over the last twenty-five-plus years. We both now find ourselves smack dab in the middle of the runway decade, and when I first shared the idea for this book, he excitedly encouraged me by saying, "I need to read that! That's exactly what I'm thinking." Well, here you go, buddy!

Over the years, I have been honored to be asked to serve on industry councils, committees, and leadership teams by industry veterans Adam Antoniades, Mimi Bock, Erinn Ford, Susan Theder, Valerie Brown, Pat McEvoy, and many others. I've learned so much from each and every one of them about leadership that I often share with clients and team members.

It took me a few years after college to realize it, but without the benefit of playing baseball at LSU for Skip Bertman, a lot of things in my life would have turned out differently. Beyond the countless memories on the field and the life-long friendships that came from it, I learned what it means to take ownership of my results and strive for excellence, how to set goals and motivate myself, and how to develop a common vision for a team. It was also there that I met baseball alum Wally McMakin, who I am grateful to for giving me my first job in this industry that I came to love.

I count it a blessing from above that at about the same time I was coming into this business in 1991, Nick Murray was beginning his career as a writer following a successful career as a financial advisor. Searching for a guide, I immediately latched on to his style of writing, and his philosophies resonated with me from the get-go. So much of the foundation of our approach, core philosophy, and perspective come from his thinking and writing, and where it is not directly attributed to him in this book, I can assure you pieces of Nick are scattered throughout these pages just as they are now even unconsciously in my brain.

I have also been positively influenced by consuming a steady diet of too many other talented writers and thought leaders to possibly name them all, but chief among them are Philip Palaveev, Steven Pressfield, Bob Veres, Michael Kitces, Mark Tibergien, Seth Godin, and Dan Sullivan.

With regard to Dan Sullivan, his Strategic Coach program has been instrumental in both stretching and focusing my thinking and propelling my personal and professional growth since I joined his program in 2008. To Dan and my long-time workshop coach and friend, Colleen Bowler, I am eternally grateful for the wisdom and entrepreneurial structure that you have shared with me, and I've tried to pay it forward to my team and other entrepreneurs.

Like Skip and Nick, Dan and Colleen showed up in my life at exactly the right time. Through Dan's connection to "Whos," I learned about Tucker Max and Scribe, whose services we engaged to guide us in this book creation process. Everyone we have worked with at Scribe has been first-class, and we are grateful for your help in pulling this book out of us. We hope this is the first of many over the years to come!

ABOUT THE AUTHORS

Prior to joining Horizon Financial Group, **Bill Bush, CRPS®** spent eight years as a CEO in the healthcare industry. He also had a lengthy career in television broadcasting, business development, and marketing operations. As a financial advisor, Bill works with a select group of individuals and families on their personal financial plans and is part of Horizon's acclaimed retirement plan division. He has earned the Chartered Retirement Plan Specialist™ and Certified Plan Fiduciary Advisor™ designations.

Doubling as the firm's Media Director, his unique background in broadcasting has been instrumental in creating unique communications with clients as well as handling media requests. He produces and manages the firm's podcast series and oversees all in-house Horizon video and content creation.

In his spare time, Bill enjoys working as an independent video producer and is actively involved in community theater. He has served on boards of several nonprofit groups, including local theaters, senior citizen groups, and community-minded organizations.

––––––

Pete Bush, CFP® is the CEO and Partner of Horizon Financial Group, based in Baton Rouge, Louisiana. He began his career in the financial services industry over three decades ago and enjoys assisting successful individuals across many walks of life in becoming more confident with their personal financial management.

Besides leading Horizon's client practice, Pete has helped build the Horizon Advisor Network into one of the largest branch enterprises of Cetera Advisors.

He is the creator of The Confident Wealth Experience® and The Confident Advisor Practice™, co-author of *The Challenges of Big League Money: Early Career*, and developer of many other creative concepts used by Horizon advisors. You can find out more about Pete and the entire Horizon team at *www.horizonfg.com*.

REQUIRED DISCLOSURES

The authors are Registered Representatives and Investment Advisor Representatives offering securities and advisory services through Cetera Advisors LLC, member FINRA/ SIPC, a broker/dealer and a Registered Investment Adviser. Cetera is under separate ownership from any other named entity. Their office is located at 8280 YMCA Plaza Dr., Bldg 5, Baton Rouge, LA 70810.

For a comprehensive review of your personal situation, always consult with a tax or legal advisor. Neither Cetera Advisors LLC nor any of its representatives may give legal or tax advice.

Individual Retirement Accounts (IRAs)

Some IRAs have contribution limitations and tax consequences for early withdrawals. For complete details, consult your tax advisor or attorney.

Retirement Plans

Distributions from traditional IRAs and employer-sponsored retirement plans are taxed as ordinary income and, if taken prior to reaching age 59 ½, may be subject to an additional 10 percent IRS tax penalty.

Roth IRA

Converting from a traditional IRA to a Roth IRA is a taxable event.

A Roth IRA offers tax-free withdrawals on taxable contributions.

To qualify for the tax-free and penalty-free withdrawal or earnings, a Roth IRA must be in place for at least five tax years, and the distribution must take place after age 59 ½ or due to death, disability, or a first time home purchase (up to a $10,000 lifetime maximum). Depending on state law, Roth IRA distributions may be subject to state taxes.

Donor Advised Funds

Generally, a donor advised fund is a separately identified fund or account that is maintained and operated by a section 501(c)(3) organization, which is called a sponsoring organization. Each account is composed of contributions made by individual donors. Once the donor makes the contribution, the organization has legal control over it.

However, the donor or the donor's representative retains advisory privileges with respect to the distribution of funds and the investment of assets in the account. Donors take a tax deduction for all contributions at the time they are made, even though the money may not be dispersed to a charity until much later.

Investing in Securities

The individuals, examples, and situations depicted in this book are hypothetical only and do not represent the actual performance of any particular investment or strategy. All investing involves risk, including the possible loss of principal. There is no assurance that any investment strategy will be successful.

Investments in securities do not offer a fixed rate of return. Principal, yield, and/or share price will fluctuate with changes in market conditions and, when sold or redeemed, you may receive more or less than originally invested.

A diversified portfolio does not assure a profit or protect against loss in a declining market.

Investors cannot invest directly in indexes. The performance of any index is not indicative of the performance of any investment and does not take into account the effects of inflation and the fees and expenses associated with investing.

Investing in mutual funds is subject to risk and loss of principal. There is no assurance or certainty that any investment strategy will be successful in meeting its objectives.

Exchange-traded funds and mutual funds are sold only by prospectus. Investors should consider the investment objectives, risks, charges, and expenses of the funds carefully before investing. The prospectus contains this and other information about the funds. Contact your Registered Representative to obtain a prospectus, which should be read carefully before investing or sending money.

Variable Annuities

There is a surrender charge imposed generally during the first 5 to 7 years that you own the contract. Withdrawals prior to age 59 ½ may result in a 10 percent IRS tax penalty, in addition to any ordinary income tax. The guarantee of the annuity is backed by the financial strength of the underlying insurance company. Investment sub-account values will fluctuate with changes in market conditions.

An investment in a variable annuity involves investment risk, including possible loss of principal. Variable annuities are designed for long-term investing. The contract, when redeemed, may be worth more or less than the total amount invested. Variable annuities are subject to insurance-related charges, including mortality and expense charges, administrative fees, and the expenses associated with the underlying sub-accounts. Investors should consider the investment objectives, risks, and charges and expenses of the variable annuity carefully before investing. The prospectus contains this and other information about the variable annuity. Contact your Registered Representative to obtain a prospectus, which should be read carefully before investing or sending money.